The Thief and the Gift

Finding Understanding and Peace Amid a Degenerative Illness

Deborah Wagner, Ph.D.

Copyright © 2024 by Deborah Wagner, Ph.D.

All rights reserved. Published in the United States of America. No part of this book may be reproduced or transmitted in any form or by any means, graphic, electronic or mechanical, including photocopying, recording, taping or by any information storage or retrieval system, without permission in writing from the publisher.

This edition published by Highpoint Life.
For information, write to info@highpointpubs.com.
First Edition

ISBN: 979-8-9908488-5-6

Library of Congress Cataloging-in-Publication Data
Wagner, Deborah
The Thief and the Gift: Finding Understanding and Peace Amid a Degenerative Illness.

Summary: *"The Thief and the Gift* documents the journey of a man living with an unnamed degenerative illness. Whereas many memoirs of illness focus on recovery and healing, *The Thief and the Gift* illustrates how a degenerative condition can be something to embrace and utilize for growth and contentment and not just something to mourn."—Provided by publisher.

ISBN: 979-8-9908488-5-6 (paperback)
1. Death and Dying 2. Aging

Library of Congress Control Number: 9798990848856

Interior Design by Kimberly E. Likley.

Cover Design by Sarah M. Charehart.

Manufactured in the United States of America

Praise for *The Thief and the Gift*

"Dr. Deborah Wagner presents a moving tribute to a man as he and the family navigate the ravages and impact of disease through time. So many themes are subtly presented and explored in the book and so many beautiful metaphors are offered to help the reader in understanding the experience of his illness in a poignant and helpful way. The journey of psychological healing is described perfectly, as Dr. Wagner describes the connections with past and present events, helping the protagonist achieve inner cohesion and growth. The descriptions are wonderful in assisting people to understand the benefits of psychotherapy when encountering such debilitating, long term diseases." – **Tamara Sofair-Fisch , psychologist**

"This book delves into the main character with such perception of his honesty, his gusto and his love for his family. You will fall in love with the main character and with the author. She has captured the depth of his soul and the true nature of a hero!" – **Michele S.**

"A breathtaking story that takes the reader on a journey of unimaginable challenges, trapped but free. Feeling the human spirit in its highest form take shape, as a daughter's unwavering support and love helps her father forge a path forward during unimaginable challenges and limitations to an examined life of meaning and wisdom. This is a journey of growth and self-awareness between both father and daughter." – **Lori W.**

Dr. Wagner is a consummate psychologist whose approachable manner and developmental perspective provide holistic care for her patients. She has particular expertise in terms of the interaction between physical conditions and mental health. In addition to her supportive style with patients, Dr. Wagner is a psychologist's psychologist with her colleagues. – **Dr. Ralph Dell'Aquila, ED.D., psychologist**

I worked with Dr. Wagner in her private practice at the beginning of my career. Working under Dr. Wagner was one of the best things I did as a budding therapist. Dr. Wagner is calm, direct, knowledgeable and is able to guide all her patients to better themselves. She engages every patient with empathy, understanding, utilizing her extensive background and education. – **Katie Gately, LPC, BCBA**

Contents

Acknowledgments	
Foreword	
Introduction	1
1 After All Was Said and Done	5
2 Traditional Man	9
3 Supper	13
4 Cat Hater	21
5 Traveler	27
6 Mortality	33
7 Enter the Thief	39
8 Bicycle	47
9 Emotionally Silent	53
10 Protector	61
11 Modesty	71
12 Fall	77
13 Metamorphosis	87
14 Simba	91
15 Ice Cream Soda	97
16 Fear or Fight	103
17 Hit and Run	109
18 Fighting the Fight	117
19 Peaches	125
20 War	133
21 Persimmons	143
22 Transition	149
23 Introspection	157
24 Success	167
25 New Old Man	173
26 Reflection	179
27 Finding the "After"	185
28 49th Hour	193
29 Stupidity	197
30 Overview of Life	203
31 Ending	211

To My Owl

Whose wisdom is profound and who never stopped learning.

Acknowledgments

Although only my name appears as the author of this book, there are many others to whom I am grateful for their direct or indirect contribution to creating it. As an author who is also a psychologist, I am grateful for knowledge I have gleaned from the many researchers, fellow psychologists, medical, spiritual and religious thinkers, and scholars who have addressed the concepts surrounding suffering, spiritual growth, and the confronting of end of life issues.

I am grateful to my brilliant friend and colleague, Tamara Sofair-Fisch, who has always been supportive of me and showed even more for this project.

The trust my patients have placed in me in sharing their experiences and emotions has allowed me to better understand the human condition. They have given me both insights into and wisdom in seeing what transpires behind the veils of defenses with which so many struggle.

I thank my friends and colleagues who were willing to read my emerging manuscript while reflecting, guiding, and emoting with me. A special thank you to Lori Wagner, whose encouraging words and support were more than I deserved, and to my husband, Steven Grundleger, who patiently listened to endless iterations of every paragraph.

My publisher, Michael Roney, along with his editorial staff, skillfully guided me into fine-tuning this book and helping me find the right words to bring this narrative to light.

Finally, and most importantly, I am eternally grateful to Him, the hero of this book. He listened to my reading to him every written word, correcting and approving as his story took shape in these pages. He is a wise and thoughtful soul whose willingness to grow, to learn, and to share his deeply moving life story with me changed me forever. Hopefully, his story will be an inspiration to countless others as they live and age through the passage of time. In his words, I wish us all "a life well lived."

Foreword

Tamara Sofair-Fisch, Ph.D.

As our population has aged, we have witnessed an exponential growth in the rise of physical and neurodegenerative diseases and illnesses. These illnesses create profound challenges to the individuals suffering from the debilitating declines in physical and mental functioning. Additionally, family members share the challenges of caring and supporting their loved ones, even as they personally struggle with the myriad impacts of the declining capacities of their loved ones.

In *The Thief and the Gift,* psychologist Dr. Deborah Wagner presents a heartwarming portrayal of a man as he struggles with the onset and transition of living life while challenged with one such illness. This man is the center of his family, and we see the impact of the disease on him and the family members who surround him. He and the family navigate the ravages and impact of the disease through time.

This book subtly presents and explores many perspectives: seeing the man and the family through the lens of a small child's eyes; seeing the impact of the patient's diminishing physical abilities and its impact on family members; seeing a young daughter's view of her father shift from adoring girl to mature woman who assists her elder's psychological growth as they journey through this disease together, and more.

Many beautiful metaphors help the reader in understanding the experience of this illness in a poignant and helpful way. My favorite metaphor was to refer to the illness as a "covert thief" who swoops in suddenly and cruelly absconds with yet another ability which so defines the self. The person is then left to develop a new self-image and sense of self without the lost ability. Then, once this is achieved, The Thief strikes again, absconding with yet another ability, and forcing another repetition of redefining the self yet again and again.

The Thief and the Gift also perfectly describes the journey of psychological healing; Dr. Wagner illustrates that even as the body fails, the mind can thrive as it makes connections with past and present events, helping the person dealing with the illness achieve inner cohesion and growth. The descriptions are wonderful in assisting people to understand the benefits of psychotherapy when encountering such a debilitating, long-term disease.

Introduction

How do we learn to live when the end of our time is in sight? This is the question at the heart of *The Thief and the Gift*, which documents the journey of a man living with an unnamed degenerative illness.

Whereas many memoirs of illness focus on recovery and healing, *The Thief and the Gift* illustrates how a degenerative condition can be something to embrace and utilize for growth and contentment and not just something to mourn. Drawing upon my years working as a practicing psychologist, this story takes an intimate, introspective look at one of life's developmental stages we almost never tell stories about.

Written to be inspiring, uplifting, and deeply empathetic, *The Thief and the Gift* is a story we know well, but don't often tell. Although it addresses the life of one man, referred to as "He" throughout the book, His struggle applies to a wide contingent of men and women as they confront challenges as ordinary as aging or as complex as navigating a debilitating illness.

The story unfolds as "She," the protagonist's daughter, seeks to help Her father traverse the transition from a strong vigorous "man of the body" to a fragile, helpless "man of the soul," as a degenerative disease ("The Thief") ravages His body. My aim is to shed light on how beauty can evolve in the face of tragedy as we explore painful topics with loved ones. She opens up previously forbidden topics with Her father, who in turn, impresses Her with his wisdom, as the opening quote in every chapter reflects.

When The Thief first visits our protagonist, what it steals away is barely noticeable. But as time marches forward, and our protagonist's body continues to deteriorate under The Thief's covert missions, it becomes clear to our protagonist, His daughter, and all who know and love Him, that life will never be the same. His daughter, a psychologist, enters this painful and confusing reality with Him, and together they explore, confront, and share the journey, fleshing out the deeper meaning of life and redefining what is and is not important. They root out the lessons offered early in life that can be revisited and utilized when events take unexpected turns, resulting in a new definition of self.

It is my wish that this narrative will be an unexpected lifeline for those readers who have also arrived at the end of their days and for the loved ones of those suffering their declines. Whether someone has a devastating illness or is experiencing declines typical of advancing age, there is much to be learned from this story.

A profound reflection on the nature of life and the period we know as "death," I wrote *The Thief and the Gift* with the aim of immersing you in a striking story that challenges everything we think we know about the end.

Chapter 1
After All Was Said and Done

"G-d blessed me and gave me a long life."

It was exactly ninety-eight years, five months, two weeks, and one day since He had entered the world, a red-faced squalling infant, drinking in His first breath of air and observing the world around Him. He felt the comfort of the arms of His loving mother as she put baby to breast. Not by word, but by instinct, He had entered into a pact with her to embark upon a meaningful life. Neither mother nor infant had the vaguest concept of how quietly, yet profoundly meaningful it would be.

As the fog cleared after He awakened from His morning nap, He saw His daughter sitting on the edge of His bed. He smiled to see Her there but that quickly faded. His face became serious as He realized they were alone, giving Him the only opportunity to explore the swirling questions that plagued His pained mind. "Why am I here?" He asked.

"Are you asking why you are alive?" She responded.

"Yes, why am I alive?"

"Why are you asking me this question?" She needed Him to give Her the direction in which He sought to travel with Her.

"I give only grief to my caregivers and my family," He replied, recalling the sleepless night before as His challenging medical condition caused disruption and concern.

"Grief is the other side of the coin that is love. You can't have love without grief," She explained.

"I never thought of it that way. That helps."

She went on to make sure He understood the entirety of Her message. "You have paid your dues up front. You have spent your life working hard to support and protect your family. You have empowered us and given us good values. You have helped me develop ideals and ethics and identities you believed were worthwhile. You sacrificed so we could benefit. Now the time has come when you need something from us. I could never pay back what you have given to me. More importantly, it is a gift for me to be able to do something, anything, for you, and I do it lovingly."

He mustered what little strength He could manage and reached up to stroke Her cheek. It was only by bending down to reach His unfathomably weak outstretched hand that She could create the desired contact. He told her, "You have made me feel so much better."

She gifted Him with Her most sincere answer. "I am so grateful and am so blessed to have you." They both cried as His hand rested on Her shoulder and Hers on His cheek, and He replied, "I am so grateful to have you. I love you."

Without a moment's hesitation She replied, "I love you, too." He hesitated with the evident difficulty of expressing what He wanted to say next. She waited, knowing that what He will say will be meaningful and will resonate within Her. He was contemplating Her flight back home; She would be taking off in a painfully short amount of time.

After more than a few moments, He spoke. "This may be the last time we see each other."

She knew what She knew and what He needed to be reassured of. "When you leave this world, you will still be here, loving me, watching over me, and protecting me, as you have always done. I will be looking for you and we will find each other; death will not separate us."

And She knew He felt the comfort of this as He looked at Her through His old, rheumy, tear-filled eyes and smiled, and so did She. She kissed Him and left, considering how both pain and beauty can exist in the same space of time and emotion; how truly accurate Her words were that love and grief make up the two sides of the same coin; and that one can choose, as He always did, to remain positive and keep the loving side of the coin facing up.

Chapter 2
Traditional Man

"Them were the days!"

He was born in an era of worldly chaos, sandwiched between the two great wars. Brought into the world with the type of poverty that does not make men into victims but instead instills a drive and an ethic to better themselves, He learned hard but valuable lessons at an early age. He grew up strong and powerful, but not in the manner one would easily recognize. He became a good man, a solid man. No one knew this outside of His community, but you might say He was a hero. He was not the type of hero who wears capes and tights and rescues damsels tied to railroad tracks. He was a quiet hero, the type who lives silently among others with His values in all of the right places while never imposing His will on others. Only those who know Him personally understand this about Him.

He was smart in traditional ways but also in ways that allowed Him to get ahead in His world, which required what one would call "street smarts." He had a razor-sharp affinity for numbers, along with an incredible wealth of acquired knowledge. He was religious in a proud and practical way, but the spiritual eluded Him.

He had lived many good years and a good many years. He was a man of the body—not vain, but connected to His physicality. He was made strong and powerful, though not overtly muscular, simply by living and doing all He had done over the course of His life. This man of the body had always kept Himself fit and trim. He was not particularly large, although one would consider Him tall. He was handsome, but never vain.

He had exercised daily before anyone had heard of doing a "workout," and when the only places to exercise were at home or a local schoolyard. Every night, after a long day at work, this regimented man performed His routine of jumping jacks, sit-ups, push-ups, and various other floor exercises engineered to keep Him healthy, fit, and strong. So when He showed up one day with a stationary bicycle, everyone was perplexed at what this contraption was. Eight miles a day was His goal and He met that goal every day. Without a doubt, He had ridden around the globe several times in equivalent miles. He did not think of it in such terms, but He was strengthening and protecting His heart—a heart that would later become the essence of all His being and all He had left.

One could say He was a traditional man who lived in a time when blue jeans were called "dungarees" and only worn by farmers, comics were called "funnies," men wore white shirts and black slacks to work every day, often with a tie, and women stayed home to tend house and raise the children. Men didn't work excessive hours. A reasonable forty- to fifty-hour workweek was all that was expected or required to be considered a responsible provider and an honorable head of household. He faithfully exceeded this expectation and worked long, hard hours, as His work ethic dictated.

Truth be told, He never really was the head of His household. That job was left to "The One He Chose," His partner whom He loved with all His heart and for all His life, the one who challenged Him to grow and improve upon Himself, even though she never knew this.

He knew what He was supposed to do and He did it without complaint. This became one of His defining characteristics. Throughout a lifetime full of reward and fulfillment, He had experienced His fair share of hardships, but one would never know, for He rarely uttered a word of dissatisfaction. When life presented those difficult moments, as when He caught someone trying to steal from Him, He confronted the would-be thief, recovered His belongings, and went home to brag about how He had outsmarted the other. He had found ways to bring humor to the situation and turn Himself from what others might see as a victim into one who had encountered an amusing or meaningful experience. And it was this part of His character that got Him through some of the most challenging experiences anyone could face.

Chapter 3
Supper

"The routine of a day was so lovingly remembered."

Time passed and He lived His life. He enjoyed the spoils of life He had worked so hard to acquire, one of them being His passion for eating. From the time She was a young child, She was fascinated by His ability to consume a meal and leave His audience stunned by the simple yet powerful performance He effected, all without conscious awareness. Every long day at work ended when He came home to a meal at the table. The One He Chose, by no stretch of the imagination a chef, prepared simple food on simple dishes. He ate alone after all of the others had long since finished their suppers and moved on to evening activities.

Each evening played out in the same manner. She would hear the door open and He would wearily enter. He called out "I'm home" as if this were an event that was not already noticed.

His routine was always the same. He would climb two

flights of stairs to find the bathroom. He would relieve Himself and then wash His hands and face vigorously. Finally, He would take one flight of stairs down and enter the room for His meal. By that time, She would be seated directly across the table from his place. The One He Chose would place His plate of food in front of Him. As He picked up the utensils, He seemed unaware that his intake of food was in fact a performance He did not know He was about to execute. She, who did not care much about food, was ready for the fascinating experience She was about to witness. Not a word was uttered, but the unspoken hunger and eagerness to embark on this nightly passage was palpable. His dark-brown eyes locked upon the small mountain of food set before Him and He began the stated performance by slicing off a chunk of steak, and with blinding speed, deposited it in His mouth.

She was intrigued by how He would always load onto His fork more food than was reasonable for a single mouth, but somehow that orifice would continue to widen, accepting as much input as He desired. The broken tooth in front, the result of a childhood accident, was no impediment to His pleasure. This was not a greedy or sloppy action; it was necessary for the eagerly sought desire to partake of that which He so thoroughly enjoyed.

Often, people choose to show their pleasure in the

most obvious way. He did not. He simply experienced the pleasure and it emanated from Him like a burst of sunlight. One bite of steak and the world was wonderful. The next forkful scooped up some vegetables and a small mountain of mashed potatoes, which was enjoyed with as much gusto as the first bite, and was always followed by a giant swig of soda. No matter how many times She witnessed this, She was always amazed at how He could swill half a glass of the beverage in one swallow.

Bite after bite, drink after drink, He continued the performance, occasionally peppered with an utterance of pleasure, until His appetite was sated and the meal consumed. While His mouth neglected to smile due to its preoccupation with savoring His treasures, a smile issued from Him, nonetheless. She sat transfixed, never truly understanding how food could be such a source of pleasure and so completely transformative to His weary self. Perhaps the desire to understand this is what kept Her coming to the table every night to both witness and enjoy the same performance. The props were different but the storyline was always the same. Every show culminated the same way: with an enormous belch, the vibrations of which could be felt throughout the entire house, and His fists pounding on the table in an infant-like display of delight while He smiles and asks, "What's for dirt?" Translation: "What's for dessert?"

Not infrequently He surprised everyone with a pre-performance show that brought "All Who Loved Him" into an excited frenzy. On these days He would come through the front door laden with packages and calling out to everyone, "Come to the kitchen!" Of course, all had to wait until He completed His washing ritual. He was a man of habit and rarely did He vary. The energy and excitement were barely contained until He returned to delight everyone with His treasures. She was excited, too, even though She had little interest in what the packages contained. It was His pleasure in sharing and being part of it that delighted Her the most.

His pride in His acquisitions was palpable as He emptied His packages. He extracted item after item, excitedly directing All Who Loved Him—"You, get a knife"; "You, get the butter"; "You, get the cutting board"—as delicacies emerged one at a time.

Wedges of exotic cheeses would appear that He deftly cut into wafer-thin slices, each passed out to All Who Loved Him for a taste. "Black bread," as He called it, known by all else as pumpernickel, was sliced off in thick chunks, lathered in butter, and doled out piece by piece. All Who Loved Him were expected to indulge in these culinary delights and All Who Loved Him did, simply because to not do so was completely and totally beyond

His comprehension, and All Who Loved Him could not bear to cause Him any disappointment.

It was hard to decipher the greater pleasure: that of the food itself or sharing it with The One He Chose and All Who Loved Him. The grand finale came when He foraged into the bottom of the package to produce an enormous bar of milk chocolate, larger than any you could find in an ordinary grocery store. With a combination of interest and excitement, after the deliverance of every morsel, He asked of each, with the expectation of only an affirmative answer, "Do you like it? Is it good?" He was incapable of believing that any human being could respond with anything other than an emphatic agreement, despite wrinkling up their noses earlier at the smells and tastes of exotic cheeses not meant for an undeveloped palate.

Perhaps even more of an event for Him was the Saturday night pre-performance show. He was so excited to develop the palates of All Who Loved Him to be in tandem with His own that the enthusiasm was contagious, in spite of the more questionable tastes of these particular treasures. Saturday nights brought the "appetizing."

The performance rehearsals began in the late afternoon when His friend sent the box of delicacies to Him at work. His friend, whose livelihood was selling such delights, proudly shared what was left over from the week with

Him. Always on Saturday, always in the late afternoon, the deliverer came with the box.

"He always made sure to bring me a variety."

"It was like manna from heaven."

"I was getting something infinitely better than what I could get in the local shops."

And the excitement would begin to course through Him as He began to salivate with the anticipation of what lay ahead. It was difficult for Him to decipher whether the thrill was greater for what He was soon to partake of, or for what the others would experience. Throughout His long journey home, She knew that He was imagining the delight He would encounter as small bodies jumped up and down waiting for the treasures about to be unpacked.

Again, He would emerge through the door laden with packages. Every item was wrapped individually in layers of paper, the likes of which one never encountered outside of this experience. Lovingly, and with the same barely contained enthusiasm as during other pre-performances, He would unwrap each item. The waxed papers contained the oily dressings of the finest of the fine, culturally relevant, and emotionally imbued varieties of fish. Each in turn was lovingly unwrapped, inspected, and presented: baked smoked salmon, whole whitefish, finely sliced lox, herring, sable, mackerel, and whatever else struck His fancy that day, and all were laid out as the feast of feasts. All Who Loved Him eventually learned to appreciate what He loved, in spite of the unblinking eye of the white fish that bore witness to the whole affair with far less enthusiasm than He felt.

He had a passion for food and He showed love to those close to Him by sharing what He so enjoyed. Even when the tongues of those He loved rejected the tastes of what He offered, their souls rejoiced, for the soul knew what the mouth did not. Instinctively, All Who Loved Him understood that this was one of very few ways in which He was capable of showing His love while no one could foresee the challenge this would eventually become.

Chapter 4
Cat Hater

"Include my flaws…that I was arrogant and intolerant."

While He was capable of great love, He was also capable of great hate, but that was limited to only one creature who roamed the earth: the cat. This might seem like an inconsequential issue, but it was of nearly cataclysmic importance. She experienced this hatred and intolerance of the innocent feline nearly as a betrayal of Her selfhood, for equivalent to His hatred, and probably even transcending it, She loved and adored the same. She saw the feline as a sort of completion of Her being, which only grew as She grew.

It was painfully clear to anyone who knew Him that there would be no contact with any feline, neither directly nor indirectly. If it were up to Him, there would be no feline residing in a household that He truly headed. There would be no coaxing of a stray to come visit with offerings of scraps of food or a bowl of milk. In sum, there would be absolutely, positively, no tolerance for any feline in His life in any manner of imagination one might hope for, much to the disappointment of The One He Chose and All Who Loved Him.

In what one may consider a miraculous moment, in some sort of negotiation that couples enter into, The One He Chose secured the opportunity to possess the simultaneously desired and despised creature. Eventually, this expanded to two when the much-loved cat went out and found her own sort of love, which resulted in yet another loathsome tiny feline (unfortunately, the only surviving member of the litter).

For all He was capable of giving, He was neither able nor willing to give in this particular area of affection. There was zero tolerance for any sort of contact or proximity to the detested new members in His life and environment. Not the pleas, begging, manipulations, nor efforts to convince by All Who Loved Him made the tiniest impact on this man, who had a stubborn streak as wide as the Grand Canyon. He would regard these detested creatures as the most unwelcome intruders in His life and His home.

Never could He have imagined the infinitely more loathsome creature that He would be forced to contend with decades in the future. Nonetheless, at this point in time He would not touch them, nor look at them. There was an unspoken agreement between the two species that a respectable distance between them be maintained at all times.

There is one thing that is critically important to understand about cats if you are going to reside with them. They understand their humans better than their humans understand themselves, and certainly better than their humans understand them. She, who loved Her cats dearly, knew this and worked in tandem with Her cats' needs, giving and receiving in a nearly psychic connection. He made the mistake of regarding them simply as animals, to be directed according to His will. Hence began the battle between feline and human.

You see, His passion for food was quickly deciphered by the feline. The feline felt it, understood it, and used it to her advantage. She was cunning and knew how to take advantage of this wise man who chose to be ignorant about her species. When All Who Loved Him gathered at the dinner table, so did she. This feline had the ability to communicate with her eyes, directed only at Him, without a sound uttered so that she could partake of what He so enjoyed and shared with All Who Loved Him.

The threat was there, subtle but very present, and He came to understand this. Grudgingly, He would throw her a scrap far from His chair to appease her and nullify the threat. All would relax and He would return to the ecstasy of consuming His meal. This cycle was to be repeated several times until the performance was complete. This was how it was every day.

The One He Chose was most unhappy with this arrangement. She warned Him, "Do not feed her at the table." He replied, "I don't want her near me. She'll leave if I give her a bite."

"You don't understand cats," she responded. "She'll keep coming back for more." It was more than He could tolerate to assume that a mere cat could be outsmarting Him. But truth be told, He kept throwing bits of food and she kept coming back, fastening her knowing gaze on him, waiting for the next morsel to sail across the divide between them. While He averted His eyes from her eyes, He feigned a blasè attitude of indifference. Meanwhile, her feline eyes bored into his being, invoking a restlessness that no one dared suggest was fear.

At some point, He was forced to realize He was no longer directing this show and made a decision to regain control. No longer would He be threatened into sharing His treasures with this lowly creature. When she came to him with her visual request, He ignored her. He thought to himself that He, in His infinite wisdom, would show them all. This was His grave mistake, for this creature who was perhaps one twentieth the size of Him, knew she had the advantage, solely because she had figured Him out, and He had not done the same work regarding her.

Now her request became a demand, but He was determined to maintain control. His underestimation of her was his undoing since she knew Him with a cunning that would have impressed Einstein. She created the rules. She sat by His side, and with the intense glare of which only a feline is capable, she warned Him.

He ignored her threat, and that was His second mistake. She knew the time for a showdown had come. There was no possibility that she would be banished from sharing in the culinary delights along with the rest of her family. This man, who could not tolerate the proximity of or contact with a feline, was going to be taught a lesson. This feline, who had never shared a millisecond of physical contact with Him, leapt up with perfect precision and landed square in His lap.

All Who Loved Him witnessed panic, horror, terror, and disgust wash across His face as He bolted up from His chair, catching the edge of the table with His leg as He did so. The cunning feline took flight as the table, laden with treasures, flipped up on its end, contents flying everywhere. All Who Loved Him were buffeted between shock, compassion, and total hysteria as they watched food, dishes, silverware, feline, and human scatter.

It could be said this was a humbling experience, although He would never acknowledge it as such. All Who Loved Him, the feline, and He knew who had won this battle of wills, but no one dared say it out loud. The feline had delivered a lesson in humility and had gained the respect of many, perhaps even Him. Compassion for the downfall of the cat hater allowed for the silence thereafter, wherein not a single person present allowed a snicker to issue forth. From that day forever more, the cunning feline received her portion of the treasures, thrown far from His chair.

Chapter 5
Traveler

*"This brings back events I've forgotten about.
I can see them, hear them, taste them…"*

Most people are travelers of one sort or another. This might lead one to think of visits to exotic destinations all over the globe, but this is not necessarily the type of traveling all people enjoy. People travel in various ways, seeking their own personal destinations. Traveling allows an individual to explore experiences outside of their immediate surroundings in the hopes of exposing themselves to that which allows growth of one sort or another. One can certainly travel in the commonly conceived modern notion of visiting foreign lands, but travel can also transpire in a purely metaphysical manner. People can travel forward or backward through time utilizing the well-tread vehicle of reading books; others may use traditions to reacquaint themselves with foregone cultural experiences. Whatever the purpose or the method, the exploring individual will seek methods by which to expand their horizons, create their own version of timelessness, and expand their understanding and comfort of themselves in the world.

He was a great but unique traveler in His own pursuits. He did have a few favorite vacation destinations that He partook of regularly, but beyond those, He had the opportunity to see parts of the world but didn't visit many. This was not because He did not have the time or the means, for He had both. It was because His travels took Him in other directions.

He grew up in an era during which different cultures sought their own enclaves. During periods of increased immigration, due to whatever hardship in their home countries or whatever promise this country offered, immigrants built communities in which they could comfortably maintain their traditions, languages, and old and valued heritages. There was some amount of mistrust and prejudice between the enclaves, primarily a result of ignorance and unfamiliarity rather than any sort of hatred, but the people of these diverse communities became familiar with one another through their work.

He embraced these different cultures via the road He enjoyed and was most familiar with: their native foods. And this was how He traveled.

She, who did not have an adventurous palate, declined

to savor the gastronomic delights brought to The City by the wonderful array of newcomers. He delighted in bringing All Who Loved Him into The City frequently to visit each enclave and discover the best of the best they had to offer His inquisitive palate. For Him, the annual street fairs were heaven-sent. He inhaled the aromas as He navigated amongst the many food stations until He was dizzy. For a man so determined to embrace it all, He was left with no choice but to sample it all. It was not lost on Her that what She viewed as alien and suspicious, He embarked upon with mouth-watering excitement. "Taste this," He would entreat. "Just a little taste; you will like it."

She assessed these new, unfamiliar foods with the appropriate suspicion of a child. "No, I don't like it." The well-worn question every parent has asked followed: "How do you know if you never tried it?" Never in His wildest dreams could He conceptualize that this was anything other than a wonderful gift offered by those from another world simply to fill the belly while making the mouth dance with savory pleasure. Never could He conceptualize that it may be unpleasant for Her to sample strange smells and alien-looking foods so far beyond Her preferred hamburger doused in Her singularly favorite brand of ketchup.

In the end, He achieved a moderate victory as She

allowed the tiniest of tiny crumbs to pass through Her tightly clamped lips. She achieved Her own victory as She exclaimed, "It's disgusting!" before the crumb made contact with a single taste bud. He believed that Her response must be hiding the true appreciation for the delights He had shared and it was only Her childish ribbon of stubbornness that forced the rejection of that which was truly beyond any such reaction.

Still, over the course of years, Her palate began to blossom as His enjoyment became infectious and her own wariness of the unusual and atypical lost its edge. The creamy-centered cannoli of Little Italy, dishes with savory sauces from the German restaurants resounding with oom-pah music, and the crusty edges of the thinly sliced yet soft-centered Spanish potatoes eventually became foods She enjoyed as well. He researched painstakingly and brought Her and All Who Loved Him to the "hidden gems"—eateries that prepared exquisite renditions of the authentic global cuisines He loved so much. He wanted to eat where the natives ate.

For the most part, this worked out very well until He decided one Sunday evening to venture to a restaurant deep in the heart of Chinatown. He diverged from the well-vetted agenda He typically prepared and chose, instead, to follow the locals into their restaurant of choice.

This was not your typical Americanized Chinese food. This food was authentic, and He was excited for the anticipated expansion of His culinary experience. When they were served their wonton soup, replete with floating cephalopods, All Who Loved Him shrieked in horror at the thought of ingesting the creatures. The only protection against total humiliation was that no one other than All Who Loved Him, and He, Himself, understood the embarrassing nature of the things they were saying. Even He did not resist when All Who Loved Him ran from the restaurant.

Chapter 6
Mortality

*"I dream about my childhood friends
and the experiences I had with them."*

For years His life carried on much in this manner. He enjoyed His food, His travels, His family, His exercise, and His friends. Once a person had earned their way into His inner circle, they were under His protective visage indefinitely, with few exceptions. This applied to His boyhood friends, who retained that status from the age of eight until death. This serious and self-important group of twelve eight-year-olds had named themselves The Simbas. On a lazy Sunday, He explained to Her that the reason for this identity lay in the fierceness of the lion with whom these little boys, who believed they were anything but little boys, likened themselves. When any one of these skinny, scrawny-armed boys looked into a mirror that reflected the distorted image He needed to perceive, He saw, as boys of this age are so myopically able to see, a strong and powerful man, ready to fight the evils of the world.

One Simba in particular was His best friend from childhood through adulthood. The two men were paddleball companions who engaged in a regular routine of playing one another in the local schoolyard every Sunday morning, followed by a visit to His home. His friend was the lucky fellow to whom He had allotted one of the two hours in His week reserved for self-indulgence. It was no wonder that once He had moved from the inner city after He wed The One He Chose, many others followed and settled within blocks of where He made His new home. This included His siblings, parents, and several of The Simbas. This magnet of a man had that sort of propensity to draw people toward Him. It would be hard to find a single one He repelled. When one day She pointed this out to him, He replied, "You make me out to be some sort of a hero." He mulled over whether to be flattered or miffed at this portrayal of Himself. She knew what He was. He did not. She knew He did not really want this sort of self-awareness because it would bring him outside of Himself and to know Himself as others knew Him. That was not what He wanted.

People who had the fortune to know Him adored Him in a manner that never wavered. Once you knew Him, you liked Him forever. That was just the way it was. He had a hearty zest for the pleasures that life had to offer. For the most part, He had an easygoing nature, but one never to be pushed too far. This was something She learned, and it took only one event for the lesson to sink in—something that happened when She was at that conflicted age of emerging from childhood into the era of the teen who suddenly discovers She knows better than everyone.

The event that cemented this knowledge happened one morning as He was sitting in His gray leather chair with nail studs peppered around the perimeter reading His morning paper, as this man of routine did every day after completing His breakfast. This was the same as His father had done, in that very same chair, in another home entirely, the only difference being that His father smoked a cigar while doing so. His chair was turned toward the window as He leaned back with His feet up and resting on the windowsill. This is where you would find Him every single morning after breakfast, occasionally nursing His second cup of coffee that He preferred to drink at a temperature that would have scalded the delicate tissues of any other mortal's mouth.

She ventured into this sanctuary with some sort of complaint about a pair of pants. She had had an expectation; He had had another. She replied with a great deal of sass and ilk that is intrinsic to that particular stage of immaturity bordering on maturity. He was a man of tradition, especially insofar as respect for one's elders was concerned. More than a bit of unpleasant discourse was exchanged when She, in her hormonally-driven irrationality of self-righteous adolescence, threw the disputed pair of pants in His face.

What transpired in the following moments was one of those situations in which one's perceptions communicate with lightning speed to one's brain, which in turn communicates with equal speed to one's limbs. She saw the fury flicker across His face and knew that a sacred line had been transgressed. He knew She had trespassed over that same line and both simultaneously experienced the transmission from sensory input, barely skipping over conscious thought, to a surging of motor activation. Each experienced the rush of adrenalin that set two bodies in motion in an amount of time too minuscule to be measured.

Luckily for both of them, She had the edge, whether this was attributable to her youth or to her fortunate upright posture as compared to His reclining, no one could discern. As in when a cat is being chased by a dog, She fled from her infuriated pursuer and in some feline-like way, hid herself until the danger had passed. Both being of a nature commonly referred to as "stubborn," each believed in the righteousness of their position. A line was drawn, the gauntlet was down, and the showdown began regarding which will was going to bend first to make amends.

It took thirty days, exactly one month of these two mulish individuals mutely circling each other until She finally broke. She knew from that moment forward to carefully stay a safe distance from that sacred line, not because of fear but because of the damage it created in His sense of honor.

So, time moved forward with the ups and the downs and the ins and the outs of life. The incident of the adolescent and the pants was long forgotten, but only by Him. Incidents such as that have a unique way of changing one's life in a most profound manner while not impacting the other in the least. And so it was with them.

And then, at a later time when Her adolescence had long since been conquered and life had again achieved a regular sort of rhythm, a day arrived in which the first of The Simbas suddenly closed the final chapter of his life at an age far too young for the others to comprehend. The Simbas had all mistakenly viewed themselves as somewhat indestructible, as they had all been young men of the streets, hardy and too savvy for an early demise, or perhaps any demise.

Saying goodbye to His lifelong friend opened a door through which He and His friends now had to travel. He, as was His nature, did not indulge in outward displays of grief. He received this incomprehensible news with His jaw set and His lips clenched and silent. The water that threatened to seep into his eyes knew to find another passage from the windows that would reveal an unfathomable reality and a pain that no Simba had ever learned how to manage. Boys turned into men, and defined by their stoicism, were victims to barricades they themselves had erected.

Without ever noticing the passage of time and the waning days of their youth, they had moved into a phase of life less characterized by self-assured invincibility and more identified by the vulnerabilities of aging bodies. They knew little about how to proceed as such, but fate had already decided that herein were lessons He would be forced to learn.

Chapter 7
Enter The Thief

"Freedom from worry comes only to those who are helpless to have any control over their lives."

When one forgets to notice, life has a way of unfolding itself in its own ways. Sometimes this happens in tandem with what one wishes, and sometimes it does not. Sometimes life unfolds in ways contrary to what one wishes. Sometimes life knows better than the human intellect what the best pathway is, leaving us to wonder why what is, is.

He was not one who was inclined to pontificate on such theoretical thought. He was more of a man-in-the-moment sort of person. As life happened, something within Him gifted Him with the ability to see the positives. Now that He was past the challenging years during which pants were unexpectedly thrown in His face while He was trying to enjoy a cup of coffee and read His morning paper, forcing Him into postures of strength and authority (and not realizing that such occasions provided the showdowns preceding middle age), He was able to pass through time.

And time for Him was marked by one of his most prideful purchases: His space-age watch.

After a particularly enjoyable vacation to a destination that offered impressive bargains in the form of duty-free products, He proudly flaunted to All Who Loved Him His new, very indulgent purchase. As He stretched out His arm and rolled back His sleeve, the metallic silver, unearthly-looking timepiece emerged. "Look at this watch! It winds itself and it is guaranteed to keep perfect time…within a fraction of a second!" This miraculous timepiece, designed by scientists unleashing the space-age technology, was most certainly of the future in an era when watches were painstakingly hand-wound daily in order to keep the time.

His enthusiasm was infectious as He strapped the watch around each thin little juvenile wrist in turn to allow All Who Loved Him the momentary experience of jetting into the future. He instructed each to "shake your arm, move your wrist, and observe the tiny arrow spinning to wind on its own." Just as He was emphatic that All Who Loved Him taste his exotic foods, so must they have a turn at experiencing this delight. What All Who Loved Him knew was that He was not impressed by items meant to impress. Whatever it was about why this watch so enthralled Him forever remained an enigma. For years He did not tire of sharing His fascination with this watch. He wore it daily, allowing it to wind itself and keep its perfect time, well past the evolution of watches that became electronic, scientific, and fitted with batteries, chargers, and all sorts of gizmos and novelties.

And He lived, marking time with His watch, enjoying the simple pleasures of a good year, as well as the ups and downs of business, a vacation with family or friends, and the most precious pastime of seeing the various outcomes of one's many years of effort and dedication come to fruition. He continued to be strong and was always one who projected the picture of (and was in most regards) in good health.

Having laudable, unwavering values, He was not tempted by, nor did He succumb to vices, except for a somewhat brief affair with cigarettes. He rarely drank alcohol. She could not remember him drinking a beer other than the moment when He ordered one while listening to a German oom-pah band during his foray into foreign cuisines. Not a soul could attest to His spending an afternoon watching a sport on the television, gorging Himself on foods void of nutrition, or becoming captive to any of the vices that commonly seduce men. He was loyal, sound, responsible, and subsequently, healthy. One might conclude that His choices regarding what to include and exclude in His life might make Him seem like a bland person, but nothing was further from the truth. His passions were all there, present, and shared in His unique way.

In this way, He passed through the years of bearing witness to the growth and maturation of those He had brought into the world. He had created and launched His family. He had auspiciously overcome the challenges and, while He never would have acknowledged it, the worries of being a sole provider in a world that geometrically multiplied what one must acquire in order to be considered successful.

Perhaps this optimistic parlaying with the challenges of life was not, as you already have observed, His only positive attribute. One ought to heed the unknown and certainly be wary of the unfathomable. This is not to imply He was ignorant of unpleasant potentials, for He had certainly suffered His fair share of such difficulties in life. However, it must surely be said that He had a penchant for viewing life on the brighter side.

So, after many well-lived years, far fewer than it seemed but far more than He had thought, The Thief found Him. By this time, two more of The Simbas, one of whom was His best friend and paddleball buddy, had moved to the other realm. This was a particularly difficult loss, for He and this friend had shared a most significant part of their lives together. His friend's final words to Him, whispered in His ear after a medical event left half of his body without the ability to function, were "no way to live." And then he didn't.

This was one of those events that was nearly impossible for Him to comprehend. This friend was far too young, too vital, and too invincible to be the victim of an untimely end. He told Her, "I was the last one he spoke to," and within this mixture of horror and honor, He was comforted to know that His friend had shared his last words with Him, his lifelong pal. And now He knew, while not consciously thinking about it, that He, along with the other Simbas, were all vulnerable.

It was during these several years that, unbeknownst to Him, The Thief had been hovering on the edges of His being, not truly making its appearance, but beginning to formulate its plan for a slow, insidious attack. One must understand something about The Thief. To call it a monster would be a gross understatement. The Thief defines cruelty. It is genderless. It is inhuman. It is relentless in its quest to utterly and completely maim and destroy. Its purpose is to decimate everything in its purview, whether that is mind or body. Nobody knows where The Thief comes from. Nobody knows how to get rid of it. Nobody knows who its next victim will be or why.

The Thief was so hidden, so subtle, and so sly, that

no one paid attention to the minimally detectable signs that it had arrived in His world. Still, even if it had been otherwise, it wouldn't have mattered at all. The Thief had an agenda and it was unstoppable. Had anyone told Him, He would not have believed them. He still allowed Himself to believe He was invincible. In fact, He had created a sense of invincibility shared among the other Simbas. Although three had left this world, they did so with a measure of choice and a great deal of arrogance that contributed to the illusion of their invincibility rather than depleting it.

Clicking. That was the first indication The Thief was present. When He was still, one could hear a very quiet but steady clicking—the clicking of the metal bracelet of His space-age watch. While The Thief manipulated time to its advantage, its port of call via His watch evidenced a cruel irony. The clicking of the watchband was The Thief's heartless announcement that it had found its point of entry, an entry through His most valued possession, which foretold the heinous nature of this opponent. The heinous, insidious plan was unfolding.

Initially, no one worried much. He had learned The Thief was there on the day He was diagnosed with a progressive, debilitating disease, but All Who Loved Him, and He, Himself, believed The Thief was weak, harmless, and capable of only minimal damage. They believed The

Thief was not wise or powerful, and that He was strong enough to prevent any harm The Thief might want to inflict. That was who He was; that was who The Simbas were....until they weren't.

Chapter 8
Bicycle

"It's better to give in if you know you're wrong than to remain stubborn."

With the loss of His dear friend and subsequent tear in His retina, His tenure of weekly paddleball came to an end. Ingrained with a nature that was exquisitely adaptable, He bought Himself a bicycle and enjoyed this substitution. This time, the bicycle was not stationary but had two wheels, and the miles He traveled allowed Him a change of scenery. Always driven to tend to the maintenance of His body, He rode daily as long as the weather was not an impediment.

Early one morning, as routine in this highly regimented man dictated, He decided to take His bicycle out and go for a ride. He had chosen this to be a part of His daily activities now that the world considered Him old, a description He would not have applied to Himself. He was still a man of the body and still very much connected to His physicality. Exercise was not a necessity but a way of life.

He did not seem to notice that the world had caught up to Him. He seemed not to recognize that most people He knew now rode stationary bicycles that were given fancy names. He did observe that they also used all sorts of machinery that directed people to attend to their bodies by moving, lifting, and contorting.

He had planned a pleasant and uneventful bicycle ride this morning. However, He was vulnerable to that which was lurking unseen. It was on this early morning ride that The Thief crept into his life a second time, but in this case, instead of merely making his hand shake, it impacted him directly. He was unaware that The Thief had silently attached itself to the bicycle with the sole intent of causing trouble.

As He rode, enjoying the pleasure His body regularly experienced when He fed its need to be nourished in this physical way, He inhaled the warm, sweet air and marveled at how others on bicycles now found the pleasures of the body that He had always understood. He was a perpetual optimist perfectly balanced with the advantage of also being a realist. He would confront what required recognition, digest and cogitate on the situation, add in a healthy dose of "positive," and deliver to Himself or another an appropriate course of action.

So, on this lovely day He allowed Himself the pleasure of

getting lost in His thoughts about how good life was. It was this very act of lowering His guard that gave The Thief its opening. The Thief struck swiftly and powerfully, sending Him careening and crashing to the ground. While those around him quickly came to His aid, the understanding that The Thief had struck Him directly left Him terribly shaken. The Thief had bypassed the psychological defenses He had erected against it, and He was shaken because there was the nascent beginning of a realization that The Thief was more of a foe than He had allowed Himself to consider.

After He allowed Himself to be helped up, He took an accounting of the scrapes and bruises left by flesh meeting concrete, and He seated Himself back on His bicycle. He delivered profuse gratitude to those who had stopped to help him—all apparently completely unaware of The Thief's lurking presence. That was His way. The division between the internal and the external was vast, as the internal self was not feeling what one would call "gracious." His internal self reeled with embarrassment and self-righteous indignation at succumbing to such an assault. This was going to require the implementation of the methodological manner with which He was so successful when confronting similar historic unpleasant realities.

Not one to ever avoid a good fight, He was determined

to not allow The Thief to get the best of Him. The Thief had power He had underestimated, but He had huge reservoirs of strength and determination that could be tapped into as this war escalated. This would not be the first time He would draw upon such strength.

He recalled one such time, a lifetime before, as a young soldier, when He was in a terrible predicament. He was proudly serving in the Air Force division of the U.S. Army during World War II. One fortunate day, which became unfortunate and yet fortunate again, He was given orders from His commanding officer that He was entitled to go home on leave. One would think this would be a risk-free situation, especially in comparison to the rigors of being a soldier in a time of war, but such was not the case. To help Him get home for His leave, He was offered the only available seat: a seat located in the gunner's blister in the tail of a bomber—a small and exposed compartment that was completely segregated from the rest of the aircraft.

Not taking the chance of missing a moment of His time off, He, without hesitation, agreed to accept this unorthodox transportation home. This particular flight was dedicated to transporting officers, all in their formal military garb, to a meeting in Washington, D.C. All went smoothly as He entered and was locked into the blister from the exterior of the plane, as was the necessity for this particular seat. The plane took off, and within moments the engine malfunctioned and smoke started to pour out. The engine was on fire.

Two issues were of the utmost concern: Would the plane crash into the marshes it was currently flying over, and would its belly full of fuel explode? Post haste the flight was aborted and the plane returned to the runway with all elite passengers on board taking flight on foot. In their excitement and fear, everyone forgot about the young soldier, bolted in the gunner's blister from the outside, frantically watching all who could rescue Him run for safety before the plane might explode.

Pounding on the glass and yelling for attention was futile as no one could possibly hear Him. While desperate to be extricated from a potentially horrific death, He can say with certainty that He was not afraid. His composure and logic dictated He must find a way to secure His safety rather than indulge in the extravagance of panicking. This mindset, so typical of Him, held until one of the officers gathered his wits and ran back to the plane with a ladder to extricate Him from His imprisonment. His legs were already running long before His feet made contact with the ground, carrying Him away from the danger.

Some would be traumatized, others incapacitated, but He added this experience to the repository of His life's story, which He proudly shared with anyone who needed a tale of strength and courage to fortify their own, or was just in need of some entertainment. He used this experience to deepen the reservoir of strength and optimism that many decades later would provide The Thief with one very strong opponent.

Few who knew Him understood the strength that dwelled inside of Him, so when The One He Chose saw the condition He was in when He finally returned home after His encounter with The Thief on His bicycle, she was determined to prevent another such incident. He was ready for a fight and knew that on His next ride, He would outsmart The Thief. After all, He had His "street smarts," His wealth of acquired knowledge, and the strength of a body resulting from years of attention.

But a next ride was not to be. The Thief now knew it could create havoc on these bicycle rides, and so The One He Chose, whose entire being was wrapped around His welfare, discarded the bicycle. All Who Loved Him agreed, except She, who, due to His influence, had become a woman of the body. She understood what impact this would have on Him and She was concerned, for although She was a woman of the body, She was more so a woman of the soul.

Chapter 9
Emotionally Silent

"The ideal man is the one you go to with a problem and He will solve it."

After The Thief absconded with His ability to ride His bicycle, He was a bit lost. He had long since lost the weekly enrichment of paddleball, only to now lose the substitution for that loss. She was rightfully concerned. What becomes of a man of the body when He can no longer live up to that characterization? How does a lifelong methodology maintain itself when the tools of the methods are removed? She knew this consciously. He knew this instinctively. Neither one of them gave voice to this new reality. Neither one of them addressed this dilemma. Both of them, because of who they were and what they understood He needed, felt the pressure to fill in the empty space left behind.

His options were limited. He was not a man of the water, but one of the earth. He tried the modern equipment in the "gym" that was not really a gym to one born in His era. He was underwhelmed by this form of exercise and quickly lost interest in it. Enlisting the aid of machinery, adorned by gadgets and knobs, hoists and levers, was incomprehensible to one whose body lived in tandem with movement and the forces of the earth in order to be strong and vital.

He was not a man inclined to run. To his mind, running was not a sport nor was it an activity unto itself. To run, one needed a purpose, a purpose with intrinsic meaning. One either ran toward a certain something or away from it, but it was the epitome of ridiculousness to simply run for the sake of running.

He *could* still enjoy a good walk. Unfortunately, The One He Chose was not one for walking. His longstanding joke to her was, "You only have legs for putting on stockings," discarding the reality that "stockings" were an item of clothing that had passed from popularity decades in the past.

When She, who was now a woman of the body and of the soul and used Her legs for more than donning stockings, was with Him, She encouraged him to walk as an opportunity to connect both of them with His soul. She understood that when a man of the body can no longer be that, He has but one direction in which to travel, and that is to emerge into a man of the soul.

He was certainly a man of opinions and knowledge. He had an impressive talent for humor and would easily express Himself in that realm. However, He had never been one to indulge in the verbal expression of thoughts or emotions. In addition to a vault of acquired experience and a wealth of well-earned wisdom, discomfort, pain, concerns, and fear were the types of things He held tightly inside the locked vault of Himself.

> "Growing up I always loved my uncle. My father and my uncle were not only close as brothers, but also lived in close proximity, which I found very reassuring. My uncle has always been a man who is kind, steady, and easy to talk to. His love of life and family along with his inner strength has never been more evident than in his long-term battle with the relentless and cruel progression of his illness." —K.W.

Long before She invited Him for their first walk, She understood this about Him: Never, ever had She heard Him acknowledge experiencing a moment of pain. Even when He walked bent over from the agony of sciatica, He never winced or complained. Nor, when questioned, would He acknowledge more than a minimal ache before shifting the attention onto some topic He deemed more worthy of attention. She recognized that in the course of living one's life, one experiences pain. That is just the way it is, yet that was not what He reflected.

He never missed a day of work due to a cold or a virus, and He made sure nobody else knew when He was sick. He remained a strong man, a stoic man. To All Who Loved Him, He remained invincible…until He wasn't.

The same characteristic that can be admirable in a person can also be very limiting, and this was how it was for Him. The stoicism that prevented Him from speaking of discomfort also impeded Him from speaking of love. Love and caring, which were present in great abundance in this stoic man, found their unique ways of surfacing to a limited level of communication, but it was complex and awkward and easily missed if one was not careful to find it.

This does not imply He did not feel. Of course, He was as capable as anyone else of experiencing great pain as He was of experiencing deep love or great emotion. But He was incapable of expressing any of those in a way that was easily recognized.

This stoic man of the body expressed His tenderness in seemingly untender ways. Rather than capitulate to a desire to hold the hands of All Who Loved Him, He would grab one young, childlike hand and say, "Squeeze my hand as hard as you can." The young hand would squeeze and squeeze with all its might. He would smile at the great but futile effort of the youngling, ending the engagement with a short, perhaps too strong of squeeze in return, evoking a yip of discomfort and defeat as knuckles crunched against one another. The one He selected for this encounter felt more the privilege of being chosen for this expression of affection masquerading as a contest of strength, than for the loss at the factitious contest of power.

For The One He Chose, it was a bit different. Not knowing what transpired in their private moments, which one would assume opened doors that were locked in the presence of others, including All Who Loved Him, He would grab her knee and give a squeeze. The squeeze was always a bit too strong and she was left wondering whether He just was unknowing about the power of His own body or if His expression of affection always had to be tempered by an affirmation of His masculinity.

He had lived in His comfort zone, maintaining the stoicism and masculine posture of withholding emotions that was characteristic and even admired in the era and culture in which He was raised. All Who Loved Him and The One He Chose tolerated this strength, which may have really been a weakness in Him. Why they did so is a reflection of what was communicated in ways not typically utilized. Perhaps the unwrapping of a herring or the brandishing of a chocolate bar laid the foundation for tolerating his knuckle-crunching, knee-squeezing portrayals of affection. But perhaps it did not.

Regardless, this was for too long a time accepted by Her but was never adequate. She wanted to hear His feelings and savor them, to keep them for Her own so She could draw upon them as She needed. She also wanted access to that inner sanctum that was highly defended but quite unsophisticated, which left Him with a serious vulnerability in the presence of The Thief.

She was a married woman before She heard Him utter the words "I love you" to Her. This was neither a spontaneous nor a comfortable event. She, who was one to always push toward verbal expression, confronted and eventually extracted the much-desired expression of His feelings for Her. She was a sensitive soul and always sought contact with the deepest part of those She encountered and cared about. She needed words and discussion of feelings, something very much alien to Him.

All Who Loved Him were not the same. For them, it was enough to know the love was there, expressed in His own awkward and unique ways.

While filled with more than moderate trepidation, She sought to break through the time-honored code of manhood, and together, She and He did.

She demanded, "Do you love me?"

He felt cornered. He squirmed as would a mouse in the face of a mischievous cat. How was He to manage this moment in which He was approached directly and firmly and expected to venture into this alien world of emotional expression?

He thought to Himself, "I must answer," but how does a stoic, traditional man of the body allow Himself to appear soft? So, He straddled Her world and His, and He answered, "Of course, I love all of you." This was entirely inadequate in that it barely strayed outside of His carefully protected defenses of hidden emotionality.

She threw down the gauntlet. "I am not talking about all of us," She challenged. "I am asking you about me!" He hesitated for a moment in which the internal battle was visible only to one who had an eye that sees more than most. Then He uttered the sought-after expression of His feelings for Her. She greedily took them inside of Herself and never let them go. More importantly, She saw the hardship it was for Him to produce that which was so alien to His nature, and She knew He produced it simply because He knew how much She needed to receive it.

So, when She invited Him on that first walk, She believed

and hoped She could gain access to that which She feared would end up forever locked inside His vault. She knew Him well enough to understand that all The Thief had thus far taken, and all The Thief was about to take, could not be managed by the stoic masculinity that had served Him so well up until then.

Chapter 10
Protector

"It was my responsibility to make sure no harm came to my daughters or my wife."

When the walk was underway, She asked Him about how He was coping with what The Thief was continually taking from Him. By now, The Thief had absconded with His ability to ride His bicycle and to steady His continuously shaking hands that were still only when He slept. The Thief had also begun ever so subtly to drain his unflagging energy. Perhaps most upsetting, worthy of implementing quite a defensive structure, was that The Thief was sapping His strength, the reliable source of His manly pride.

When She was just a girl, He'd flaunt His strength by saying to Her, "Make a fist and punch me in the stomach as hard as you can." This obviously was quite contrary to the message a typical parent impresses on a child.

She thought to Herself, "Hit my father? How can that be okay? This must be some sort of a trick…a setup," but She knew that was not who He was. So in Her disbelief, She asked Him if He really meant it.

He insisted. "Hit me as hard as you can." So She balled up Her girlish fist and plunged it with all of Her might square into His gut. With trepidation, She looked up to meet His gaze, afraid of what She might see. Would there be pain or anger reflected in those familiar brown eyes? Surprisingly, they were smiling and proud as if they were saying, "See how tough your dad is?" Had She taken a moment to consider before meeting His gaze, there would have been no doubt about what She would find there because when that juvenile fist met His abdomen, it felt as though her knuckles had just been thrust into solid concrete.

This little exercise of triumph over an aging body became a game that was replayed many times over the years. She knew that with each and every thrust of Her fist, His pride at His male prowess was reinforced. So, when The Thief began its siege into His physical hardiness, His ego and His faith in that which He was always able to rely upon, was in jeopardy.

On this walk, She was determined to push through the cursory and dismissive attempts at engagement that were typical for Him when dealing with emotional subjects. He had always avoided the acknowledgment of pain or discomfort, perhaps because He saw it as a sign of weakness, perhaps because it opened a vulnerability He was unwilling to consider.

She recalled the time long ago when He appeared at the breakfast table with bruised knuckles and was reluctant to even acknowledge a physical injury, regardless of the fact that it was visible to All Who Loved Him. It was a bit of a challenge to get the story, which ordinarily He would be proud to share, due to it being contrary to the wishes of The One He Chose.

He knew, as All Who Loved Him hammered Him with their entreaties, that He would be forced to explain the reason for His bruised knuckles in the presence of The One He Chose, who was not very happy about this incident. As it turns out, He had been in some sort of traffic quarrel—the type that tends to escalate quickly when the drivers are both men, the opposite sex is present, and a man's mind dictates He assert His machismo (which The One He Chose never did care much for). The two drivers had blustered and puffed, and once the foolish other made a snarly comment about The One He Chose combined with a jab to His shoulder, the foolish man's unfortunate jaw met with His fist.

Although The One He Chose disapproved of the encounter, she could see the barely hidden pride He took in this showdown and affirmation of Himself as a man who would always protect those close to him.

This was yet another defining characteristic of His. He was not afraid to fight for what was His, for what He believed in, and for who He was. The fight was not always physical, but if such an altercation were required, that was what He would deliver. And He taught this to All Who Loved Him. There was little All Who Loved Him could do to engender a sense of shame in Him, but the one thing they understood was the enormous pride He felt when they exhibited a similar stance in the face of an unrighteous offense.

This was important to Him. He often shared His story of being confronted by a superior officer in the army who demeaned Him with a prejudicial slur. One does not need to be well-schooled in the affairs of army hierarchy to understand the consequences of disrespecting the rank of a superior officer. But He had a different hierarchy—that of righteousness. After His initial verbal challenge to this foolish clown parading as an army officer failed to elicit a conciliatory response, the officer found himself embroiled in a physical altercation that ignored the rank of an organization in favor of that of decency, delivered by a man who stood by this with all of His being. The end of this story was a miracle in and of itself, for He was not court-martialed nor disciplined in any way—but did receive a clown's apology.

Lest you mistakenly deduce He was a brute who had a preference for finding excuses to wield His fists, you must really understand the heart and soul of Him. His religion, His family name, and His loved ones were all under His protective visage at any cost. The fight of fists was the last option for an egregious offense.

This principled man, this protector of what was His, carried out His duties earnestly, solemnly, and at times ridiculously. Understanding the "why" and the "whatnots" was not a prerequisite for honoring the decrees of All Who Loved Him.

There were times when a situation called for the use of other weapons of protection, as on the day She got married. The man She had chosen for Her betrothed was someone He not only approved of, but also liked. This was somewhat an anomaly, for He tended to keep a wary distance from any male that had in common with Him what He knew men desired of women, especially one of His. Nonetheless, these two men, one young and idealistic, the other older and wizened, had developed, perhaps due to an unspoken commitment to protect what was His, a friendly, respectful relationship that did not once evoke any sort of masculine posturing, despite the fact that the betrothed stood a solid four inches taller than Him.

As a practical woman, She was aware that She was about to wed a very fine man who happened to have one troubling flaw: he was habitually late. This was a concern She was not willing to confront on her wedding day, so She, in her own calculating way, told Her betrothed to be present at the home two hours before it was necessary. She reckoned this would deliver him right on time. Her betrothed, wisely choosing to begin on the right foot what would be a very long journey together, arrived precisely at the requested time, a full two hours before anyone had any use for him.

This created a bit of a dilemma in the household because The One He Chose and All Who Loved Him were busy with wedding preparations that included primping and preening and pandering and pampering that men do not understand, but are an absolute necessity, complete with traditions and superstitions, for women.

The betrothed was at a loss for what to do with himself during all of these goings-on and found himself with an invitation to join the father of the bride as He dressed in His bedroom. Both men were not truly themselves, in a daze of sorts, one because he was about to marry, the other because She was about to marry. The betrothed was already in his wedding garb, and having nothing else to do with himself, joined His almost father-in-law as He prepared himself for this life-changing event. The enormity of what was to transpire left the men oblivious to the state of undress in which He was at the moment: in His boxer shorts devoid of wearing anything else, not even His socks.

The betrothed wandered over to the window, partially absentmindedly and partially reflectively, as the two men engaged in idle but awkward chatter. Without warning, and seemingly without reason, He assaulted the betrothed from behind. The betrothed found himself blinded by a pair of socks, each sock balled up and firmly planted over each of His eyes by a very agitated father of the bride who was, with great effort, trying to shove him out of the room. The betrothed, clearly confused and quite alarmed, was experiencing one of those moments when the mind reacts faster than reality and thought of the insanity of this man into whose family He was about to commit His eternity.

It was not an easy feat to keep those socks planted on the eyes of the tall young groom while He, in his boxer shorts and with great effort, pushed and maneuvered the younger one until He was removed from the room—all without offering any explanation. The betrothed allowed himself to be handled in this manner, perhaps because He saw no other option, or perhaps because in such a circumstance it is best not to try to understand. It was only once he was completely removed and safely placed outside in the hallway that an explanation for this offensive and seemingly insane gesture of protection was offered to him.

Not a sentimental or superstitious man, He respected those attributes in All Who Loved Him. As She prepared for Her once-in-a-lifetime event, She had left instructions that everyone must prevent Her betrothed from viewing Her or Her gown before the marriage was to take place. The two befuddled men had been chatting directly in the company of the wedding gown that was hanging in the room, pristine and wrinkle-free, waiting for the moment it would be put into service. Suddenly, He emerged from His fog and realized His mistake in inviting the groom into the vault that housed this bridal treasure. He had to protect Her because that was who He was. And with a pair of socks, that was the first and last time in His life He ever protected that which was His to protect.

So, decades later, when She took Him for that first walk and She broached the topic of His current challenges, She encountered the barriers of His history, those that stood for His stoicism and His masculinity. She knew He viewed Himself as the one who protected, as All Who Loved Him and The One He Chose viewed Him, not the one who was in need of protection.

In the uncomfortable exchange between them on that walk, they were both aware that the actions of The Thief were forcing a reversal of roles between child and parent. In an effort to maintain the status quo, He indulged in denial of this reality and He parroted the words of others: "This is a minor challenge...not too bad...it can be managed...The Thief can be held at bay."

She knew that He would suppress any concerns or fears that might arise as He confronted The Thief and its brutal agenda in service of His posture to protect The One He Chose and All Who Loved Him. She was determined to set a new course with Him, defying the time-honored avoidance of addressing such painful topics. She would not be quieted with platitudes, so with the delicate skill such as a surgeon would possess, She began Her operation to excise whatever festering emotions might lay beneath the surface. Her precision assured Him of maintaining His stoic posture while excising the hidden wounds inflicted by The Thief in its quest to take that which did not belong to it. She knew this would be an operation that would unfold over the course of many walks and many talks, Her determination fueled primarily by Her desire to travel beside Him on this very arduous journey.

While one might say He was solely engaged in the psychological defense mechanism of denial, those who knew Him understood that this was His typical optimistic way of approaching life's challenges. He held the belief that

He could conquer anything life handed Him, and in fact, this was not far from the truth.

Chapter 11
Modesty

*"The good that's come out of this is that
I'm more sensitive to other people's feelings.
I'm a better person."*

With the knowledge that The Thief was somehow finding inroads into the tiny unprotected crevices in His armor, The One He Chose and He realized that they must reorient themselves in time and hasten to enjoy experiences they might otherwise have delayed. They invited All Who Loved Him, which now included their life partners, to join them on a trip. Now that The Thief had set its sights on His mobility in a way that made a difference—but not a difference that was obvious enough to allow for open conversation—a dilemma presented that All Who Loved Him did not have the ability to resolve comfortably.

The Thief had not yet stolen His ability to walk but had absconded with His stamina, making walking any sort of distance quite exhausting and challenging. This was a particularly difficult reality for this man of the body to navigate. He had begun to adapt to the loss of balance and the loss of strength and function in His hands, but the reduction in the use of His legs was fundamental in that the strength of His legs represented the essence of His being a man of the body. Use of His legs had been the seat of His ability to play paddleball with His childhood friend, to walk and run stairs in the workings of His job, and to stand up to those who levied injustice upon Him and those He was charged with protecting.

All Who Loved Him and The One He Chose met in private to construct agendas of interest that would not challenge His body or His pride. No one had the courage to cause Him pain by stating the obvious, or that special accommodations must be considered in an effort to compensate for that which now belonged to The Thief and no longer to Him. Ironically, All Who Loved Him and The One He Chose should have been the recipients of the pities that were misdirected at Him. As is so common among the well-intended but fundamentally ignorant, people made assumptions about His ability to accept what was. The lack of open discussion with Him was a result of their fears and inability to accept the presence of The Thief, not His.

So, All Who Loved Him and The One He Chose colluded and whispered suggestions of wheelchairs or other mobility aides that were quickly discarded in the misunderstood effort to protect what The Thief had not yet been able to infiltrate: His pride.

The result of these secret conversations, the planning and scheming that felt exceedingly important but were ultimately unnecessary, was that they produced a joint decision (that fooled no one but themselves) to allow for shortened walks punctuated with frequent periods of rest disguised as necessities for snacking or sightseeing. They made choices for planned events by prioritizing His comfort. It was critical to All Who Loved Him and The One He Chose that He had pleasure. And He did. This was especially the case when all of the life partners of All Who Loved Him took Him on a beer tour. The One He Chose fretted and warned about respecting His condition, but this lively group was determined to make sure He had a wonderful experience. When He returned just a tad intoxicated wearing a bright yellow sailor's hat, as did the others, and an even brighter smile, no one needed an explanation. He was happy and so were All Who Loved Him.

She would certainly bathe in the warm happy memories of this tour if it were not for the cruel reality of just how much The Thief had taken that He had kept hidden. During the course of one of the secret conversations, The One He Chose disclosed to All Who Loved Him that bodily needs must be addressed with more frequency than ever before, more similar to the attention one must pay when with a young child. This was a rather delicate matter for Him, who tended toward the stoic and preferred to liken Himself to all others rather than as someone vulnerable and in the clutches of a cruel and very shrewd purloiner.

The One He Chose and She were conscientious enough to avoid infantilizing Him but concerned enough for His modesty to devise a scheme that would accommodate both. She would ask Him to accompany Her to the restroom in the hope that He would take advantage of the opportunity. All went well as the two made their way to their private destinations, while She enjoyed the few moments alone with Him. When they each completed taking care of their needs, She felt Her heart plummet into the deepest recesses of Herself as the reality of the failed mission became apparent. Even She, who prided Herself on never avoiding addressing anything that needed addressing, could not find an iota of either wisdom or courage within Herself to confront this. Instead, as they walked back to the others, She deliberately walked in front of Him to hide the front of His pants in a loving effort to protect His modesty.

This experience impacted Her in a most profound way. As She struggled to compose Herself and digest what had transpired, She felt an overwhelming sadness for Him, but that was the least of what shook Her. In those brief moments, She feared She was on the precipice of being forced to let go of the man She had always known and loved—one who always had been strong and independent. She feared that there would now be a wall, so thick and impenetrable, constructed of embarrassment, humiliation, and topics too painful to address, that would cause him to slip further and further away from Her until there was a chasm too vacuous to be bridged.

This was, perhaps, the moment She underestimated Him more than at any other time during their life together. Perhaps She also underestimated Herself, for at that moment they began their journey of ensuring that separation would never happen.

Chapter 12
Fall

*"Fight for what you believe is right.
Give up what you believe is wrong."*

The One He Chose took upon herself the duty to replace what the heartless Thief had taken, or at the very least, to take care of the functions He could no longer provide for Himself. While this proceeded relatively smoothly, it certainly presented its challenges. The One He Chose and He, too, shared a fair amount of resistance and denial as to what was really lost. All Who Loved Him shared a clearer vision of His limitations, perhaps because they were slightly removed from the situation, which reduced the emotional impact on their daily lives. Suggestions and cautions were summarily dismissed by The One He Chose, who tried to resist the emerging role reversals that partner with advancing age and poor health. The One He Chose, in defiance of her fears of loss of control, blindly and perhaps defiantly held onto the mistaken belief that He still retained that which The Thief had already taken, and this is what set the stage for the fall.

As was His habit for a lifetime, He had His breakfast and read the morning paper. Now that He had long since relocated to a warmer climate and a lifestyle more suitable for His age, He no longer had the grey leather chair with the nail studs that had belonged to His father. Instead, He had switched to a modern couch for this daily ritual.

On this particular morning, when His legs and compromised sense of balance still allowed Him to move (with some difficulty) from one location to another, He assessed Himself through the lens of His younger, healthier self and decided to retrieve His morning paper from the driveway while The One He Chose was tending to her daily ablution. So, in the driving rain, He ventured out, navigating the few yards from the living room to the driveway to obtain the desired object. Alone, and with a confidence that belonged to His younger self, He made Himself vulnerable. The Thief, who was always lurking on the edges of His being, made use of His denial and seized this vulnerability for yet another full frontal attack. The Thief swiftly grabbed the precarious traction of His feet that met with the wet concrete while simultaneously sweeping Him off balance, with full knowledge that the weakness of His body had no compensatory mechanisms to right itself. As He fell hard against the unforgiving surface, he listened to the sounds of His bones breaking.

He lay helpless, alone, and immobile as the rain pelted His freshly broken body. The Thief was smug with the satisfaction of such a great accomplishment and cruelly watched as too much time passed while He suffered in agony until The One He Chose finished her bathing and noticed Him missing.

There was a great concern among The One He Chose and All Who Loved Him that this latest attack by The Thief would leave Him permanently wheelchair-bound, but fortitude was part of his very essence. What still belonged to Him, inaccessible to The Thief, was His determination to overcome any challenge. The doctors bolted and stitched His broken bones together, and then He was handed the Herculean task of enduring the pain and finding the perseverance to make all of these parts work once again.

In challenging moments, not truly moments of despair—for He was not one to indulge in that weakness for more than a millisecond, if at all—He would draw strength from His own life's history. In this instance, He reflected on His almost superhuman feat of endurance from years before when He was a soldier, when there was yet another incident of a failure of righteousness on the part of those charged with being leaders of men.

His lieutenant, drunk with his misperceived sense of self-importance, was given the task of compensating the servicemen with their monthly paychecks. This leader, intoxicated with immorality, whose thinly veiled impotence oozed from his very being, chose to make payday a punitive experience. He forced two hundred men to stand at attention in the hot blazing sun for hours, each waiting his turn to receive a single ten-dollar bill, a five-dollar bill, four singles, and four quarters, following a salute and a statement of purpose as to why he was there. Upon completing this unnecessary formality, implemented only to feed the ego of one who must suffer from a deep insecurity that in turn created a need to demean another, each of the soldiers was asked (more accurately, required) to contribute a portion of his meager earnings to the Red Cross. Only then did the transfer of wages begin.

Each transfer of money was counted thrice, first by the lieutenant alone, second by the lieutenant into the hands of a military policeman, and finally by the MP into the soldier's hand. Every soldier had to wait until all were paid before being dismissed, and this charade always was arranged to take place on the soldiers' day off.

On one scalding Saturday after a painstaking procession of men was subjected to this offense, instead of being dismissed by the lieutenant after receiving their cash payment, the men were held back and told there was a shortage of one hundred dollars. Each of the two hundred men was asked to contribute fifty cents to make up the difference so that the lieutenant's count would be even. He, whose early life on the city streets taught Him a thing or two about a shakedown, and that thrice counted money could not possibly be short, knew what was behind this alleged shortfall of money from a lieutenant whose sense of entitlement exceeded his moral code.

So when the soldiers were asked if anyone objected to this plan, His was the singular voice who did so. He was angry, and this injustice gave birth to a fierce defiance. The drill sergeant called Him out of line and accused Him of being stingy to which He replied, "I'll show you how stingy I am," and proceeded to take two of the four quarters He had just been given and throw them hard and fast into the distance, propelled with unearthly speed not by the army-hardened body but by the indignation that only the morally offended can muster.

As might be expected, His action was powerfully received. The reversal of humiliation from lieutenant upon soldier to soldier upon lieutenant was felt through the ranks of men like a rolling thunder. It took a full thirty minutes, during which time He was forced to stand at attention, still in the blazing sun, for the lieutenant and his drill sergeant to conjure a penalty for this breach of willingness to accommodate the lieutenant's dishonesty.

The punishment was heavy-handed. The decree was to force Him to run three laps around the field, this following the two and a half hours plus thirty minutes already spent standing at attention in the heat. He was up for the challenge, adrenalin being His strongest ally second only to His indignation.

As the drill sergeant took sadistic pleasure in the imminent degradation of this man who was not afraid to confront a challenge and who stood for the righteous, He looked directly at the drill sergeant and reminded him that the law had a voice stronger than His, that any punishment of physical duress inflicted upon a soldier must also be taken by the commanding officer. Hence began the running of the field by two men determined to teach the other a lesson: one a lesson of intimidation, the other a lesson of righteousness.

When He finished His punishment with His defiance and righteousness still intact, inured to the scheme to break body and spirit as the lieutenant and the drill sergeant had intended, those who wrongly believed they were in power foolishly pushed their agenda to the next level. As the rank and file watched, the drill sergeant, now with the dual purpose of degrading Him and stemming the groundswell of support for His position from His fellow soldiers, told Him He must now start running laps with him around a larger field. The strength of His body coupled with the strength of His resolve provided all that He needed to meet this upgraded and vile challenge. So began the running of the larger field by soldier and abuser.

There are certain people who fail to understand that the power of one's morality will supersede the power of another's to intimidate and demean. The officers underestimated the strength of the foe they had in Him. That was proven as the drill sergeant began to falter from the physical exertion that his mind and his body were ill-equipped to handle. The drill sergeant, in an effort to preserve his own pride, told Him they would now walk the remaining laps, rather than run. He, utilizing the strength of His character and fueled by defiance, said to the drill sergeant, "You told me to run, and I am going to run." In the vain effort to avoid losing the showdown on the stage of the field, in the army, in the face of two hundred men plus officers, both men resumed their run. Only a few short yards were crossed before the drill sergeant collapsed in a dead faint, face twisted with utter humiliation, kissing the earth. This time the rumble through the ranks escalated into a wild cheer for the one among them whose actions against those who chose to abuse their power had rebalanced their humanity.

Sadly, or perhaps happily, this is not the end of the story, for there are many foolish men who will not give up even after defeat has been undeniably established. The officers were not inclined to accept the humiliation of defeat and instead foolishly chose, once again, to try to break this unbreakable man. Another drill sergeant stepped in to complete the task at which his brother-in-arms had failed so miserably. When He was called into the office of this new sergeant, whose sole purpose was to degrade Him and re-establish the order of the immoral, He, who simply was unable to withstand the unethical punitive presentation of power implemented solely to demean, was told there would be further consequences meant to eradicate His "win" and plummet Him to His rightful place beneath all else, most notably the officers.

He was told He must now clean all of the eighteen latrines, including toilets, sinks, and showers by Himself as punishment for what He "did" to the other sergeant. With courage, grit, and wisdom that transcended the intimidating situation, or perhaps because of His youth, He removed the spectacles from his very nearsighted eyes, threw them to the floor, and ground His boot into them until the glass was a pile of shards and the metal a tangled web of wire. He looked squarely into the eyes of what would have been His new abuser and explained that He could not possibly engage in such a task as cleaning the latrines with His compromised vision.

Wiser than His predecessor, this sergeant knew with whom He was dealing. This sergeant sent Him to town to acquire a new pair of glasses and told our hero He never wanted to see Him again. And that was the end of that, that is, until the face-planted, dirt-encrusted drill sergeant became His buddy and presented Him with a new uniform.

Chapter 13
Metamorphosis

*"I'd like to tell you I went out and played ball,
but you'd know I was lying."*

He and She continued their walks, albeit with increasing difficulty. They talked, and gradually the discussions of His challenges became easier for both of them. While He had been nearby for Her entire life, She began to learn that She really hadn't truly known Him at all. While She worried and suffered for his pain, there began a slowly dawning reality that He had capabilities She would not have believed possible in this mortal, human man of the body.

Sometimes The Thief skulked and stalked and garnered tidbits of His being, such as His strength and stamina. At other times it made a full frontal attack, sinking its claws into some precious or critical part of Him. When The Thief, with its sinister twisted grin of triumph, stole from Him the strength of His hands, such that completing a meal was fraught with frustration and a drastic reduction of independence, it reverberated throughout Her being as She recalled the hypnotic exuberance with which He had feasted in His younger days. After this latest assault, She expected His pride to dictate the mood of the meal such that All Who Loved Him would shrink into uncomfortable silence.

Such was not the case. All Who Loved Him bore witness to the metamorphosis that was now underway, for He knew how to maintain His pride while He simultaneously accepted that The One He Chose would have to manage the task The Thief had recently stolen from Him. As The One He Chose cut His food into manageable pieces—a ritual He would previously have found wholly unsatisfactory— She was forced into the memory of a singular evening long, long before when She witnessed an insanity of disproportionate size to what should ever evolve at any one dinner table.

As was His habit, as previously described, He would stun his dinner-table audience with the enormous forkfuls of the desired delicacy on his plate that would be shoveled into an ever-expanding orifice. The One He Chose, who by the most conservative estimates would be considered anxiety-prone, would lecture on this worrisome behavior as often as she would take a breath. Her words fell on deaf ears. From His perspective, there was not a single possibility that any caution, concern, or worry was going to interfere with the sheer pleasures that existed in His enjoyment of the feast.

The outcome of that particular evening continues to be the subject of conjecture. Who was the greater victim— The One He Chose, who watched Him turn purple as a slab of steak could not make its way down His gullet? Or He himself, who sunk toward unconsciousness as He succumbed to an absence of oxygen that was caused by a most delicious, but ill-placed, chunk of meat?

Chaos ensued as All Who Loved Him and The One He Chose frantically tried to separate Him from that which was suffocating the life out of Him. In those days before the Heimlich maneuver was broadly known, their chopping, bending, and patting somehow dislodged that mass of partially masticated food, launching it airborne until it completed its journey right at Her feet. Her eyes shifted between the steaming lump and Him, who was now enjoying the intake of air with more gusto than He had previously enjoyed the meat.

Despite this highly traumatic experience to All Who Loved Him, and especially to Her, this incident didn't change the way He consumed food—not one tiny bit. As it turned out, only The Thief had the power to do that.

With his food now dissected into child-sized morsels, He still continued to indulge in the mouth-watering sensations of the delicacies He was experiencing. He would not forgo an opportunity to dine out in a still expanding exploration of eateries, even knowing that the independence of His consuming His own meal was gone in a most public way.

When She ventured to give The One He Chose a break so that she could focus on her own meal, He did not wince at the reversal of roles or His own need for help from one He created but smiled thankfully while instructing Her as to the next preferred mouthful. Hence began that metamorphosis from the independent, strong man of the body into something other that was yet to unfold. She knew not how this would take shape, but much later on She would once again be astonished at how greatly She had underestimated what was just another aspect of His true strength.

Chapter 14
Simba

"You can't get a perfect score in parenting."

His selfhood—amorphous, sometimes hidden, sometimes broadcast but always adapting—revealed itself to have wide-reaching implications, far wider than She could have ever hoped for. She continued to find her alter ego in the company of felines, having set Herself up as a fostering refuge for hapless little kittens who happened to find themselves in a motherless situation. When a litter of little orange tabby cats came under the protection of Her nurturing umbrella, something, perhaps unconscious, possessed Her to name one of these tiny five-week-old, orphaned kittens "Simba."

He was not exactly thrilled to know that She maintained an expanding interest in that singularly loathsome creature of the earth and that He had to negotiate yet another cat-related unpleasantness, but this did not interfere with His willingness to visit and be a guest in Her home. The scope of His metamorphosis became glaringly apparent when

She, perhaps seized by what one might label a moment of temporary insanity, approached Him, kitten in hand, to introduce to Him and inform Him that this kitten carried the namesake of His childhood pride.

How can one describe the essence of a kitten, the contradictory feel of its little muscular body encased in the soft, sweet gentleness of cottony fur, or the round kitten belly filled with nourishment? How can one communicate the feeling of the tiny heartbeat that is loud, yet quiet, only to be drowned out by the compelling rumble of the satisfied purring or the pure beauty of the little pink mewing mouth? What pleasures equate to the squirmy little desires to play, immediately followed by immediate and exhaustive fatigue coupled with a trust so profound that the tiny being will drift into the deepest of sleep nestled into the warmest crevices of a human's anatomy? He certainly could not. He would maximize the distance between Himself and the tender little being, preventing even a remote proximity.

When She approached Him with the kitten in hand, His reaction was the opposite of what She expected. That would have been, at best, some sort of guttural, mumbled expression of displeasure. Instead, He offered silent, neutral, nearly approving acknowledgment of this tiny, innocent kitten with its soft trusting eyes and tiny, pink nose.

Encouraged by His minimally positive response, in another moment of insanity but perhaps more likely a sort of prescience, She invited Him to pet this being who was a member of His lifelong cast of enmity with the entire feline species. With a hand that shook so violently it could not be directed to safely navigate a morsel of food from fork to mouth, He reached up and stroked that tiny kitten's soft, very vulnerable self. To say She was amazed would be a serious understatement. To say She was flattered would not capture how utterly loved She felt by Him at that moment. What She felt seemed to traverse a universe She never believed He could exist in with Her.

She asked Him if He would like to pet the kitten again. In His guttural voice of certainty, He replied, "No."

After some time, the talks between Him and Her no longer unfolded on leisurely walks, for those were no longer possible. Truth be told, quite a bit was no longer possible. The Thief was becoming more ambitious and much greedier in what it possessed. As the strength began to leave His hands, He found that the simplest of activities were no longer to be taken for granted. The Thief, in quick succession, with malice and little regard for the one it was leaving helpless, absconded with His ability to walk without utmost effort, to groom Himself, and then shortly thereafter, to clean Himself. This man of the body, who was proud but not vain, was suddenly in a position in which He needed another to help maintain His well-protected standard of self-care.

She, who knew of His pride in having always been fastidiously clean and well-groomed enough to always appear pleasant and approachable but never excessive, gingerly began to help him with this task—opening the psychic wound She felt was oozing beneath the surface. One would think that making such a drastic transition from taking care of one's daily cleansing to having another be responsible for it would be humiliating, if not utterly devastating, but He found, from somewhere deep inside of Himself, gratitude for the one willing to take on this chore. This man of the body, rather than having bitterness for His loss, felt empathy for the caregiver. He did not complain, because He accepted the road He had to travel.

Of course, He hurt in that deeply hidden place inside oneself where indignation lives. That hurt welled up in him when an insolent caregiver, whose job it was to tend to the body that housed this precious soul, made an attempt to demean Him for being unable to tend to the most private parts of Himself with hands that no longer obeyed commands. "I will not clean you there. I know why you are asking me to do this. You can do it yourself or remain dirty."

An observer might mistakenly have thought Him broken of spirit when being ravaged by The Thief, but as the body weakened, the spirit only became stronger. He, weak in body, but strong in righteousness, angrily showed this caregiver, who turned out to not be a caregiver at all, how little of her demeaning behavior would be tolerated. "Can you see I cannot clean myself? Do you think I would ask you to take care of something so personal if I could do it myself?" That was her last opportunity to make the pretense of being a caregiver to Him, for He would protect that which was His to protect, this time that being His pride.

So, when She sought to open what She assumed was an oozing psychic wound, He shared with her His story of righteous indignation at the caregiver, and the heroics of restoring justice to an unjust situation—not unlike when He did so with the clown who believed he was an officer of the army, or the fool for whom He was willing to bruise His knuckles. And She was proud—proud that He was still who He had always been.

She learned that sometime later when He had the most respectful of caregivers who tended to the same intimate bodily needs, the situation was very different. He shared that this authentic caregiver had said "Pardon me," as she tended to his more private needs, and that He had answered her with a smile and the internal comfort of knowing He was still Himself. "My pleasure."

Chapter 15
Ice Cream Soda

*"I'm not special. I'm not unique.
I'm just another banana in the bunch."*

The secret recipe for His very much sought-after ice cream sodas was acquired in a most unusual manner. When He was a young man, long before He found The One He Chose and created All Who Loved Him, He was out in the mountains climbing laboriously to the top of a particular peak. Along the way, He heard the distressed cries of someone in trouble. He was clueless as to the source of this desperate wailing but was determined to find it. He trudged up the mountain, searching in caves and crevices, refining His echolocation until He encountered a most unfortunate man who had found himself in the sort of trouble that one cannot extricate himself from without the help of another.

This unfortunate soul had fallen into an abyss during his hike. Upon landing on the hard earth, he felt the bones in his legs fracture. With no one to help him, and searing pain shooting up his leg, he was helpless to do anything but cry out in the hopes that someone would hear him and come to his aid. His desperate cries are what united victim with savior.

He, upon hearing the man's cries, looked until He located him at the bottom of the abyss. He climbed down and fashioned crutches of sorts that helped support him while comforting him and sharing what food He had on His person. No less than two weeks passed in this shared predicament until the man's bones knitted enough to facilitate some minimal ambulation.

This injured and hopeless man had been struggling for what seemed an eternity. By the time He finally located this helpless soul, the desperate man's hope for survival had diminished quite substantially. With great effort and more than a healthy dose of compassion and concern, He was able to extricate the no-longer-troubled gentleman from his very precarious situation, whereupon He learned that the person He had just rescued was no ordinary individual: He was a brave and very honorable man who was the chief of a well-known Indian tribe; one who possessed great wisdom and power. He held many secrets, among them formulas for some extraordinary consumable concoctions.

He, who was an honorable and compassionate man, had had great concern for this chief's plight and had risked His own safety when He embarked upon the rescue. Nonetheless, He was successful in saving the chief's life. The knowledge of what this stranger undertook and accomplished to save him lost no meaning to the chief. So, with infinite gratitude, the chief said to Him, "You placed yourself in danger in order to save a stranger about to meet his final destiny. For this, you must be rewarded. An honorable man such as I must show his gratitude to another honorable man, such as yourself." And with that, the chief bestowed upon Him his treasured formula for the world's best ice cream soda.

Upon returning home, He, who we know has an appreciation for food that reaches higher than any mountaintop, immediately created the much-desired treat from the treasured formula. As He took a taste, He knew without a shred of doubt that this was, indeed, the world's most exceptional ice cream soda. He decided at that moment that He would honor the treasure the Indian chief had entrusted to Him. He would be happy to create these wonderful delights for others, but would never share the secret recipe.

And this was the story He told many years later to All Who Loved Him each and every time He made an ice cream soda for them. He reveled in their delight as every swallow of the delicious concoction brought smiles to their young faces and filled their tender bellies.

Now, one may wonder if the smiles were really about the ice cream soda. There is no doubt that the storytelling was equal if not more satisfying than the soda. You see, He was capable of weaving a story that would have All Who Loved Him riveted with fascination. When He told a story, those present found themselves witness to the unfolding event, not in thought, but in a surreal way as if they were there with Him, sharing the experience. The One He Chose was a more precise type of thinker and was frequently miffed at how the embellishments necessary to turn a somewhat ordinary event into an adventure could be so deftly interwoven in the telling.

He utilized this very same talent after "the fall" in a very different way as He lay helpless and broken for months in the hospital and subsequent rehabilitation. How would this man of dignity and pride survive in an environment in which all aspects of privacy, choice, and dignity belong to a cadre of others, and the pain of healing and regaining function was all He had left?

One of His many great strengths was His ability to accept that which was unacceptable. Knowing what was ahead of Him made it pointless for Him to complain, not that it was in His nature to do so. He suffered a great deal of pain that no one knew existed until long after He had healed. He suffered from hallucinations after His surgery. He suffered from being in an unfamiliar environment with unfamiliar people and an unfamiliar routine. He was deprived of daily meals that satisfied His well-developed palate, leaving Him to feast on flavorless, tasteless, mush called "food."

Perhaps what was most jarring for Him was sharing this experience with the sorry souls who were in infinitely worse shape than Him, those who had lost not simply some degree of functioning of the body, but the mind, as well.

This was the population of which He was now a member—those who spent the better part of every day folded over in a wheelchair, listening but not hearing, watching but seeing nothing, speaking but not ever being heard.

Due to His injuries and subsequent surgery, all of His bodily needs were, by necessity, tended to by a staff of nurses, aides, and other attendants. He was helpless, and the control of time, the privacy of His body, and to a certain extent His thoughts, no longer belonged to Him. He was confined to bed, except for the daily arduous drills meant to restore His previous functionalities, drills that, because of His weakened condition, were as grueling for Him as basic training would be for a soldier.

One would expect this to be a devastating blow to Him, He who was so very much a man of Himself. So, when She saw Him, and He spoke to Her with an openness that had become increasingly comfortable, She was relieved to hear His tales of this experience. Similar to when She was a child, She delighted as He wove His story of the bevy of female nurses who entered His room several times each day and surrounded His nearly naked body, covered only by a hospital gown that did not really cover. They indiscriminately uncovered Him to peek at wounds, measure this or that bodily function, bathe Him or shift body parts, and redress with gauzes and liniments the newly dissected pieces of Him. These committed women were intent on tending to His every need.

Rather than view this as an inordinate humiliation, He recast this experience and saw the similarity between this and the foregone fantasy of virtually every young, sexually vital man, including His own younger self, and this filled Him with a sense of humorous irony. "This is what every young man wishes for: lying naked in a bed surrounded by women," He told her. This was what His agile mind was so capable of accomplishing: ignoring the details of the unpleasant, while exaggerating those of the positive, sprinkling in a heavy dose of humor, and ending up with a story that uplifted the spirits of all who were available to listen.

Chapter 16
Fear or Fight

*"It's like fighting off the devil;
eventually the end will come."*

Painfully, slowly, He recovered from the fall. Weeks of hospitalization followed by weeks of rehabilitation followed by months of physical therapy optimized His minimal capabilities. No one knew the extent of His pain or His frustration, for He was not one to either dwell on such matters or share them. Time passed as He struggled to fight The Thief in the relentless battle for His functioning. The Thief took, and He took back. The Thief weakened, and He strengthened. There was a net loss for Him, but the battle was persistent and ferocious.

The Thief, never satisfied with small victories, decided to raise the stakes of this war it could not seem to win and went in for the kill. Still ignorant of with whom it was dealing, underestimation being its greatest flaw, it charged, nonetheless. In an unguarded moment of luxuriating in an upright position, shifting from sitting to the walker that

He now needed to aid His mobility, The Thief, with barely a whisper of momentum, swept Him off His feet and sent Him spiraling backward, breaking and cracking a new set of bones from leg to clavicle. Thus began, once again, yet another healing process.

What washed over Him in that moment of realization of this new yet old and familiar reality no one knows. To face again the insertion of pins and rods and sutures and all sorts of devices required to mend the not really mendable self was beyond what He was able to process.

While She had previously delighted in His stories, She was also aware of the subtext. She, who was quite knowledgeable about defense mechanisms and compensatory strategies, always sought to evoke an expression of what lay beneath. As much as She enjoyed His stories and took comfort in His ability to view hardships from a most positive perspective, She sought the honesty of what His innermost pain and fears might be. So with the offering of another sort of hearing, He, in their private conversations, shared with Her His utter frustration and dismay at His helplessness and how that dovetailed with trying to manage the functions over which He still had control.

This experience strayed from the prior internment, for not all caregivers actually give care. In this instance, not all who were assigned to be a part of His recovery were of the nature to encourage, facilitate, or even consider the human being that dwelled within the old, broken body. Not all saw the shining, goodhearted soul who had a lifelong commitment to fight valiantly for righteousness and was now jailed inside a body ravaged by a Thief. This seemed so sadistic as to be incomprehensible.

Sadly, He was forced into an understanding that there were those admitted to the profession of healing who did not have the ability to see beyond physical injuries. Their job was a duty.

He described the humiliation of being reduced to less than a human being. "It's a major injustice that the other patients and I were labeled as a pain in the ass and ignored," He explained. "It's a terrible feeling to be so impotent." As He continued to speak, the feelings overwhelmed Him. "I lay there and gnashed my teeth. I became enraged at the nurses' callousness as they ignored my cries for help. I'm in their hospital and they are supposed to help me, not make me worse."

He went further. "They ignore a person's suffering and inflict mental torture as they walk by and hear me and see me, yet choose to become deaf and blind, deciding not to help me."

There were no individuals in the caregiver rotations; there were only responsibilities. One cannot use the term "tending" or "caring" for patients when speaking of these automatons, who were absent a heart and a soul. In an effort toward finding an understanding of this emptiness, one can hope that caring and compassion were present at some time before man's suffering encased and hardened their ability to feel it, but that is of little consolation to the victims of their heartless ways.

What saddened Her most was that She witnessed the collapse of His defensive structure in such a circumstance. Even His uncanny ability to find the humorous in the unbearable failed Him. In utter dismay, He described to Her the rage He felt when He was forced to wait an inordinate amount of time for an attendant to come and help Him with His bodily functions, which had become increasingly urgent and uncomfortable as He waited and waited and waited.

He unburdened Himself as He spoke. "I pressed the call button as they taught me, but no one answered. I saw them walk past my door. I called out to them. They looked my way but ignored me. I saw others walk by. I pleaded for them to get someone to help me, but nobody came."

He went on. "Finally, one nurse came in. She had no time for me; she didn't want to be bothered." And then He was told by this particular nurse, who did not represent the whole of the attendants, "Go in your pants," as she walked away.

Such an insensitive response, one that communicated a complete dismissal of His personage and dignity, hit Him like a physical blow. In His fragile, seemingly helpless condition, He, in His unwavering determination to right a wrong, found the strength to pay little heed to His vulnerable circumstances and upon their next encounter gave that nurse a verbal lecture on appropriate behavior, followed by an invitation to her supervisor to ensure that nurse act in accordance. He would not allow Himself to be treated in a manner that desecrated His humanity. This not only belonged to Him but was sacred. No Thief or nurse could destroy this part of Him. He was still willing to fight for what He believed was just. She, crushed by the humiliation that was foisted upon Him, understood that He was still the man She was proud of, still the man to serve as Her role model, still Her hero.

The vulnerability of His body did, however, begin to create one of the soul. While She sat by His bedside, He explored with Her the questions that creep in to undermine one's peace of mind when one is in a circumstance such as His. Although He had rarely experienced a sense of fear, that alien emotion now began to visit him. The questions that insinuated themselves into His mind could not be swept away by a tongue-lashing or throwing quarters into a field. There was no compass of righteousness or time-honored beliefs to guide Him down this uncharted path.

He had always been one for whom time was endless, as was health and independence. Pleasures to enhance His journey through life had been fairly attainable via one means or another. If such pleasures were unattainable, all that He required was a change in perspective to feel His kilter had been righted. Now The Thief had changed all of the rules. There was no guide, no wisdom from parents long gone, no advice from trusted others who had trespassed through a similarly challenging journey, no street smarts or acquired knowledge that could illuminate for Him how to proceed and how to govern Himself. There was no roadmap for Him to seek help and support, be it physical, psychological, or spiritual.

His formula for a happy and successful life no longer fits the equation of His unfolding state of being. This was a critical part of the plan The Thief had plotted: to take away the balance of His being by wreaking havoc with His body.

Chapter 17
Hit and Run

*"I dream about my childhood friends
and the experiences I had with them."*

Life often has a way of preparing us for eventualities that we must one day confront. We can experience events as singular happenings with meanings wrapped around a unique circumstance, or we can try to extract from that occurrence what deeper meaning, life lessons, or strengths we can derive from happenstance.

Little did He know what life had in store for Him. Little did He know that what happened to Him at the tender age of eight would echo in His life decades later when The Thief made its entrance.

The lesson that was written into His destiny began in an era when neighborhoods were places where a mother did not give even a cursory concern to sending a small child out into the local world. They were absolutely safe, with good-hearted people who looked after each other's children with equanimity.

It was an ordinary, uneventful day that spontaneously changed lives when His mother sent her little eight-year-old child out on an errand. Not twenty minutes had passed before He was catapulted into a devastating and prolonged state of helplessness as a result of a vehicle versus pedestrian accident in which He was the hapless victim. Fate had its own agenda, and those involved usually have no idea what is in store for them. So, with the innocence of childhood and the ignorance of His destiny, He had proudly set out, knowing He was trusted with the responsibility of completing an important task.

Unfortunately, He left his home at the same moment in time when a sixteen-year-old miscreant chose to steal a car. He walked toward his destination. The miscreant hit the gas and took off. Neither one knew that within moments their lives would become intertwined and forever changed. The unlicensed speeding driver, seeking a thrill, spiraled out of control and crashed into the little boy on the sidewalk. When the panicked husk of a person behind the wheel realized he had the head of the now unconscious child hooked on his bumper, he shimmied the car alternately into reverse and forward, while breaking countless bones in that little body, until the intimate relationship between car and child had been severed, and the nearly lifeless and very much broken body of the boy dropped onto the street. The driver sped off to hide his cowardly, heartless self.

As so often happens in life, the evil is juxtaposed with the good. The saint who arrived upon the scene shortly after the devil made his exit gathered up the heap of devastation that had moments before been a happy little boy and rushed Him to the hospital.

He spent several months in the hospital, suffering through surgeries and therapies to stitch, clamp, tie, and altogether put Him back together. He was plated with casts to immobilize broken bones, and traction to stabilize unstable body parts. He was alone and He was helpless.

The era was one in which doctors were lords and ran their hospitals like prisons. Visiting hours were limited and strictly enforced. No accommodations were made for the tender comforts so desperately needed by the little battered child. Televisions were not yet created, telephones were something available only at the local pharmacy and did not reside in individual homes, and a video game, if even conceptualized, would have been placed in the category of science fiction. So there He lay, immobilized by the restrictions of the devices of healing, helpless to do anything for Himself. He could not stand. He could not walk. He could not take care of His hygiene. He could not bathe. He could not feed Himself. He could not entertain

Himself. He was alone practically and emotionally in His horrific torment. But that was what was necessary in order to return Him to the business of growing up that had been so violently interrupted by one who can only be described by words of moral depravity.

A lifetime later, when He shared with Her the reflections of this life-changing event, He sifted through the negatives that were most certainly worthy of expounding on, and somehow, in the manner in which only He was capable, He recalled positive memories of that time. While He hesitated to speak of the insurmountable fear and suffering He endured, He did share memories of that traumatic time—a time when a significant portion of His body was encased in casts with one leg strung up high by pulleys on the ceiling.

"One night I awoke to the sound of rain pelting my window. I was frightened and called the nurse because it was raining so hard, only it was not rain. Blood was spurting out of my forehead, arcing over my face and hitting the cast on my leg, making the tap-tapping sound like rain on a window pane."

He went on. "The nurse came in and the blood hemorrhaging from my head hit her uniform. She panicked and called for help." Terrified, helpless, and emotionally alone, the little eight-year-old boy gave Himself over to the army of nurses and doctors who rushed in to stitch Him up and stop the bleeding. Ninety years later, the scar over His left temple still tells the story of that terrifying night when the rain was not rain.

And then, He extracted what enhanced His little childhood soul, and He reveled in that. He recalled the comfort of affirming that a higher power was watching over Him, and of the reassuring words of the doctor to His mother that He would be alright. He spoke of the commitment and love of His mother. "Every day She made all of my favorite foods, filled two packages, walked to the train, rode to the stop near the hospital, and walked again until she got here. She made sure I had her homemade cooking because I didn't like the hospital food. She carried these packages to my bedside every single day so that I wouldn't have to bear any additional discomfort."

He recalled how His mother advocated and protected Him upon His return from treatment to allow Him the time and care He required to complete His recovery. He shared the stories of how a solid group of friends, subsequently named The Simbas, came to support and entertain Him as He lay with limited mobility on His road to recovery. He recounted how an ill-tempered neighbor who resented the noisy banter of playful boys turned a hose on all of them, dousing the helpless child and His friends with ice-cold water, which ultimately invoked the ferocious mama bear's emergence and taught that neighbor quite the lesson. And He lamented how a decade later, He felt the bitterness in His gullet that the subtle but present impairments left behind nearly prevented Him from serving His country.

So, how could He draw upon this ancient experience to help His current situation so many decades later, when the suffering, the loss of control over His body, and His independence from that ordeal had been supplanted by warm memories of feeling loved? Both situations, one historic and the other present, were subject to life's ironic way of transporting us through its twists and turns only to bring us right back to where we started. Both situations brought Him the helplessness of a body, broken and immobilized, and parked in an environment unfamiliar and not reliably friendly. Both situations, one experienced by an eight-year-old child and the other by an old man, educed from Him a mechanism by which to cope with the unfathomable.

Perhaps the answer lies partially in the difference between the two situations and partially in the similarity. One situation was characterized by healing and a return to health and living. The current situation was characterized by a diminishment of self and functioning that was the antithesis of health and living. In both situations, He extracted what was good and loving from devastating events. He clothed Himself in the positives that a negative evoked. In His parents' cultural tongue, He had always been taught that "a bad thing is a good thing," and this was what He lived by, then and now, believing with all of who He was that there is always something good that can be learned from anything bad.

Chapter 18
Fighting the Fight

"I sacrificed for the love of my child's animal
that I couldn't tolerate
and chose for an animal that couldn't speak."

She had listened and learned the lessons He had taught, some by example and others by the sharing of His life's stories. He had instilled within Her the desire to stand up for righteousness and the willingness to fight for what She believes in. He had modeled for Her the code to protect that which was Hers to protect, and by the time The Thief found Him, She was well prepared to fight The Thief with Him, utilizing Her own strengths.

As She armed herself for battle, primarily using Her greatest strength—that of unearthing emotions and guiding them toward an appropriate outlet—She recalled the image of Him as a hero from so very many years in the past. The day had been one of those ordinary days until an event unfolded and sent it careening into the extraordinary.

On this particular day, The One He Chose was driving All Who Loved Him from here to there when The One He Chose cried out in horror. Their most beloved family cat was lying in the road, broken and bleeding from his mouth, the obvious victim of a hit and run. The mangled heap of fur and flesh appeared lifeless. The One He Chose ushered her young into their home to protect them from the agony of viewing the devastation on the road outside. He, who felt nothing but loathing for cats, stood guard on that road, routing traffic away in order to protect the little unfortunate soul until the vet could be summoned to collect him.

One need not wonder about His motivation for acting in this manner. It would be right to assume that seeded deep within Him was the memory and accompanying empathy of having been in the very same predicament as that brutally assaulted and abandoned little being; they were two kindred spirits, one human and the other feline, destinies interlocked in a most preternatural twist of fate. It would be right to also assume that His distaste for the feline species had little to do with the knowledge that All Who Loved Him loved the cat. It would be right, as well, to assume He was then and always the protector of All Who Loved Him.

The news was not good. The cat's condition was grave.

Much was broken. He had taken a blow to the head and it was unknown whether He had sustained damage to his brain. At a time before there was such a thing as an MRI or very literally a CAT scan, far more was unknown than was known. Surgery was required to wire him all back together with no guarantee of survival or functionality. It was revealed years later that it was He who insisted on investing a substantial amount of time and money to minister to the beloved cat, rather than euthanize the suffering animal.

When queried on the reason for His insistence, He simply stated, "G-d gave life to this animal; it is not mine to take away." Perhaps there were nascent memories of His childhood experience as the victim of a hit and run that influenced His actions, but He had not a clue that the choices He made that night would create the structure upon which She would reflect, many, many years later, time and again as The Thief created its havoc.

He fought for this cat, this creature for which He had no sentiments of endearment. Years later He explained why. "What happened reflects the sentiments and sacrifices of a family," He said. "There were times I felt like I hated those cats. I was a father who made a sacrifice for the love of my child's animal, one that I could not tolerate, and I made a choice for an animal that could not speak for itself."

This was very symbolic of the love a man had for His daughter and the love His daughter had for the cat. "No sacrifice was too great," He had explained. Accordingly, She would utilize the lessons that He had instilled in Her at such a young age to fight for Him. She was of Him, and She loved Him, and She was prepared to fight.

In order to accomplish this, She first had to understand what sort of fight He needed Her to fight. By now, The Thief had stolen so incredibly much. The Thief had added to its cache of purloined treasures His ability to feed Himself, His continence, His balance, His ability to walk independently, and so many additional functions that are of a typically insignificant nature, too ordinary and detailed to ever make it to one's conscious awareness. These would be insurmountable to tally, but nonetheless significant enough to impact His ability to live His life as He had done previously. She could see the toll this took on Him, even though He tried to pretend the impact was always less than it was.

When an opportunity presented itself for Her to have some time alone with Him, She, with much trepidation, but with far more courage due to the importance of the issue, broached the question of what He wanted. The enormity of the conversation about to happen was nearly enough to send any human soul tripping over oneself to escape, but She needed to know what He needed, and She needed Him to know that He could share what He needed to share.

Quality of life. That overused cliché that represents a profound concept yet is so haphazardly thrown about was what was nagging at the edges of Her motivation to open a dialogue. It seemed apparent that He had a diminishing quality of life, and She felt that it was important for Him to have an outlet in which to share and ponder.

It was unclear, upon broaching the topic, whether He had given the concept quite a bit of consideration or whether His wisdom and approach to life was so profound that His answers emanated from the moment. The truth that He shared, His truth, was that quality of life, or what one would assume was the measure of quality of life, was nearly irrelevant to Him. This man of the body, who was becoming less of the body, was redefining not just Himself but His being in the world.

After each assault in which The Thief would pillage and plunder, He sustained a period of emotional recalibration, and not always with ease. When The Thief robbed Him of His balance and the strength of His legs, He initially resisted using any sort of supportive device to help Him balance. Eventually, He accepted that aid, this "third leg," in the pursuit of upright mobility. This was a difficult concept to embrace, but His rationale became, "At least I can walk."

When The Thief eventually ransacked His ability to walk with a cane, He resisted adopting a walker into His regimen, but again, He accepted this necessity with the same rationale. When The Thief snuck in, stealing His cane and making the use of the walker inadequate, while delighting in its cruel ability to defile and degrade, and forced Him into a wheelchair—not always, but in any situation that would require the strength, stamina, and balance of His former self that was now in possession of The Thief—He said then, "At least I'm still here."

The impact on His quality of life was negligible simply because He reduced the value and importance of every ability after The Thief absconded with it. A Freudian analyst might insightfully describe this as a utilization of the psychological defense mechanism of "sour grapes," a defense that mandates "if I cannot have it, I never really wanted it anyway," but this was not the case for Him. When His ability to walk independently was stolen, He reevaluated the importance of walking independently. He was able to recognize the importance of such an ability in another context, one of youth and vigor. That took on a new meaning in the context of His current condition. Hence, the importance of independent mobility attained a new relevance or lack thereof.

In light of this understanding, She knew that the fight She wanted to help Him fight was not one of outsmarting or overpowering The Thief. Rather, it was one of Her joining with Him as He explored and redefined the absolute truths of His previous beliefs.

Chapter 19
Peaches

> *"The best decision I ever made in life was*
> *to have your mother and my children.*
> *The second best was to join the army."*

If you have not already deciphered this, He was a man who certainly indulged in a sense of humor and more than a bit of mischief to compliment it. Brought up on the urban streets in a challenging but close-knit community, He learned from a young age to use His cunning and all available resources to survive. This wisdom came in quite handy during His service to His country.

This man of honor was eager to serve in the military and fight for His nation. His country had been attacked, and His sense of righteousness demanded He protect her. It felt as if His pride had been offended when the boundaries of safety had been breached in His own land. This privilege had nearly been denied Him due to the injuries resulting from His childhood accident, but fortune was on His side, and after a couple of attempts, He was able to pass His physical exam. Hence began His sojourn as a soldier.

Basic training was rigorous, and supplies were very limited. The young soldiers, who became lean and sinewy, sorely missed many of the simple pleasures of civilian life. For Him, the greatest deprivation came in the lackluster variety of nutrition that some, but not He, would call "food." So, when He, who knew how to seize an unusual opportunity—one He sometimes may have even had a hand in creating—found Himself and His army buddy in a position to secure some cans of peaches in syrup that had mysteriously become available, He took it.

You should understand that in ordinary circumstances, a can of peaches was not something He, nor most people, would take a risk to acquire. But in circumstances such as He was in, a simple can of peaches in syrup became a valued commodity that resonated within Him on many levels. One of those offered Him a connection to home that was then a world away. Sometimes there is that fine line between what is right and what is not wrong, and acquiring these cans of peaches lay alarmingly close to that line. He didn't take the time nor effort to determine on which side of that line this opportunity belonged. In order to have what they desperately wanted, while avoiding the potentiality of finding themselves on the wrong side of that line, His buddy and He devised a plan to store this acquired treasure in the rafters of their barracks. There, the cans would be well hidden and safe, available for consumption at the appropriate time.

His buddy and He were quite satisfied with the success of their escapade and anxiously awaited the opportunity to fetch the cache of the forbidden fruit and proudly share it with their army mates. They were quite heedful of the troubles that would befall them if discovered, so patience was essential. As they waited for the perfect moment to enjoy the spoils of their caper, the sun beat down on the barracks that were built before there was any such luxury as air conditioning. Unbeknownst to our adventurous duo, the fruit greedily absorbed the heat until the precious peaches were ready to burst forth from the imprisonment of their metal cans.

The heat continued to increase inside the rafters as the soldiers dutifully marched through their daily rituals. It was not until their daily inspection, when all of the inhabitants were spotless and polished in barracks that were fastidiously clean lined up before the inspecting officer, that the cans surrendered to the internal pressure of the fruit trying to escape. As the soldiers rigidly stood at attention, they waited and watched the officers measuring the outcome of their daily duties. A quarter was tossed on each and every bed as each trembling man waited for the bounce that would indicate it was sufficiently made. The officer inspected boots for adequate polishing and clothing for any irregularity. Meanwhile, the men stood fearing an observation of an imperfection that would be untenable in such conditions.

That was when He felt a moist drop hit His head. Without daring to look up, terrified to move to wipe it off, He realized that it was a single drop of peach syrup. That was followed by another and another.

Dread was an understatement of His internal state as He glanced from the corner of His eye to witness a slow, yet steady sequence of drops make their way onto the head of His coconspirator. Drop after drop of the pungent peach syrup made its way down as the men maintained their attentive stance, with prayers, such as they had never before made as ardently, that the officer would not take notice. Fortunately for them, this particular officer preferred to focus on the inspection of polished belt buckles and shoes and linens tight enough on the bed to bounce a quarter, rather than inspecting heads for peach syrup. Therefore, the outcome was nothing other than one highly stressful, perhaps even terrifying, daily inspection that had aroused imaginings of court martial just because of a desire to have canned peaches.

Of course, His stories were most riveting when

woven around some incident involving food. That this unfolded while interred in the army is of little surprise. He was certainly quite accomplished in bringing about a yearning to acquire whatever gastronomic delights He was describing, even if they were not truly anything out of the ordinary, such as a can of peaches. One cannot do justice to His description; this is a talent that is solely unique to Him. Whenever He described a food or a meal, one would feel compelled, in a manner that was quite irresistible, to sample that which He described.

She, who could not tolerate fizzy drinks, desperately wished She could find a way to enjoy an ice cream soda. The taste of the beverage was in stark contrast to His description of it, as was the case with canned peaches. She was unable to comprehend the incomprehensible conflict between taste and description. When He spoke of any encounter with consuming cuisine, whether or not it was truly an artful creation, the ecstasy in His eyes shown clearly. This added to the effect, making the listener's mouth water with desire as His countenance reveled in the memory of His indulgent pleasure.

What He described was ethereal. What She tasted was something else entirely. Neither He nor She could ever really understand this differential. He, especially, struggled to grasp how another could fail to experience the pleasures of what He so enjoyed. As a child with a limited palate, She was satisfied solely to ingest the stories, since in His world, love had become synonymous with the sharing of food.

She wondered if this unbreakable connection had been established long ago when He was that eight-year-old in the hit-and-run accident. Alone, frightened, and in pain for three eternal months in the adult, childless world of the hospital, the sole connection with the comforts of home was the daily packages of food brought by His devoted mother to ease the soul while nourishing the body. The vehicle for love and healing had been food, and perhaps it still was.

Now that He was in such a fierce battle with The Thief, He again needed to draw upon whatever tools and resources that had settled within Him. The concept of determination is understated when observing what efforts He made to wage a fair fight. When nerves will no longer transmit the necessary information to one's extremities, what are the options? When the mind tells the legs to walk and one looks down to see his own legs silently standing in place with perhaps a minimal jerk or spasm, what are one's options? For many, the options end with the addition of a walking aid, and eventually, mobility is only accomplished with the use of a wheelchair. For Him, this did not happen without Herculean will and extraordinary resistance. He stood. He told His legs to walk. His legs were deaf to His command. He communicated louder and louder until the message was delivered. One weak and violently shaking foot moved inches in the desired direction. Breath… minutes…the other foot moved inches in the desired direction. To witness this event was to access diametrically opposed emotions that well up simultaneously and are irrationally conjoined.

Trepidation, hope, despair, pride, sadness, and elation tied together uncharacteristically in a singular instant as one trembling foot was placed in front of the other, painstakingly, as He slowly traversed a small and eventually a greater distance. Triumphant, He would announce, "I walked! I walked all the way around."

It was no different when the mind directed the hands. Never to turn His back on a challenge, He doubled down with His directives until His hand held the fork and the fork held the food. They quaked and they tipped, and only a portion of the sought-after nutrients made it to His watering but patient mouth.

Still, He was determined. Meals seemed to take a lifetime, but He fought the fight without a complaint, without anger, without what one would expect from someone so severely challenged. He repeated endlessly the arduous action of bringing food to mouth until His stomach was full, His appetite sated.

And this was how it was with every setback, after every single assault The Thief waged, and with the simple passage of time, as The Thief continued its relentless war against our brave hero.

Chapter 20
War

*"You can't win the fight
without getting your hands dirty."*

As The Thief continued to have its successes as it waged its battles, it took into its gnarly self increasingly more of what once belonged to Him. The Thief had now tipped the scales of balance in its favor, making it even easier to win each successive battle. As it acquired more of what was once His, there was less and less in His arsenal with which to fight. His body weakened as The Thief strengthened. Even the love, support, and determination of the combined wills of The One He Chose, All Who Loved Him, and He, Himself, were fiercely inadequate against the increasing power of The Thief.

All Who Loved Him were desperate to avoid the acceptance of this changing dynamic but were forced to, nonetheless. The One He Chose and He were the most resistant to this acceptance, with The One He Chose certainly owning the position of being least able to accept the changing dynamic, and this became the fuel for the battle that ensued.

The incomprehensible yet ultimate avoidance of this acceptance initiated an effort on the part of All Who Loved Him and The One He Chose to explore and implement various methods to outsmart The Thief, or at the very least to minimize the ravaging damage it was leaving in its wake.

Throughout His life, He had always been a voracious reader. Historical fiction was His preferred genre. She could not recall a time when His nightstand was without a stack of books that waned with unrealistic speed, only to be quickly replenished after His next foray to the oft-frequented library, and this only after The One He Chose had been so inundated with books He had purchased that she put a stop to the acquisitions in favor of the copies borrowed from the library. He devoured those books with an appetite and a zest similar to the way in which He devoured a meal. So, when The Thief hijacked the steadiness of His hands, He was left without the ability to stabilize a book in a way that was remotely readable. She, unable to bear the divorce of His passion from its fulfillment, found a tray table with a stand that would slide into His chair and facilitate His connection to the world of past and present that would stimulate His mind, allowing Him to hold onto what The Thief was trying to take. This provided the additional facility of the time-honored daily perusal of His morning paper. So, there He sat in His chair, book on the table, effortlessly turning pages while successfully forestalling the sacrifice of another pleasure.

In its ruthless quest to not be outsmarted, and defeat being a concept it would not accept, The Thief then created a new plan of attack. Seeing that accommodations had been made to circumvent its previous win, it circled around its victim and positioned itself for the next assault. This time, The Thief went for the eyes. Too weary to connect sight to reading material, His eyes failed in their ability to focus on the words for more than a brief period of time.

It would be comforting to believe that He, in his well-established ability to absorb the attacks with which The Thief assaulted Him, would rebound quickly with pride and dignity as He had previously, but this was not the case. His facile mind and intellectual hunger for knowledge and stimulation were sorely threatened. He lamented to Her, barely but effortfully trying to hide the enormous pain this brought: "I can't walk without help, I can't bathe without help, I can't eat without help, and now I can't read." And that was all, a simple statement of the facts.

Her mind feverishly raced to find words of comfort. Whatever arose from her deepest empathy would land as platitudes. There was no point in reflecting on what

> "He has always been a kind and gentle soul. I am both honored and proud to have been His son-in-law for over four decades. Time spent with Him has always been a wonderful experience. I can honestly say that other than the incident in which He jammed His socks over my eyes, I have never had a moment in which I questioned His very admirable morals and values. During our years together, I have learned much about Him including His respect for others, His honesty, His sense of fairness, and how He has set standards that He has lived by. Not only would He listen and show interest in any story I had to tell, but He has always had a story to share with me." —S.G.

little He still could do. They both knew the emptiness of such a concept. He was not the sort of man who needed nor wanted trite although meaningful words of sympathy, and She knew this, too. To commiserate with sentiments such as, "Poor thing, this shouldn't happen to you, I feel so bad for you," would be nothing short of empty and most probably offensive. He was not a man who engaged in self-pity and found even less comfort in pity from others.

As to why this happened to Him…well, that was something He spent a great deal of time and thought trying to understand. There was little reason to ask what emotional fallout had been created in Him; the widening and deepening hole was visible. A sadness overwhelmed Her, but rather than fall into that chasm, She drew upon that which She had learned from Him: accept this new limitation and find a method in which to move forward in spite of it.

The machinations of the war were at full throttle. All Who Loved Him gathered their wisdom,

energized by their compassion, ignited even more so by their indignation, and fueled by His lessons that they should never accept defeat. They regrouped for the counterattack.

The singular story of defeat and humiliation that He had shared with Her arose in Her consciousness as She pondered the battlefield on which He was living. Some people who have such painful experiences in life tuck them away into a shamed and hidden compartment of their memories, hoping they will never be discovered. This was not His way. This is not to say He was a person who undertook a loss easily, for He was a proud man. He was also a very wise man who had learned early in His existence that one's defeats, especially those saturated with embarrassment, can offer some of the most valuable life lessons, becoming motivators for the exploration and acquisition of greater wisdom. This was His path when, at a tender age, those who prey on the innocence of children took something valuable from Him but unwittingly gave Him much more.

He had just experienced the honorable ceremony that officially granted Him the status of manhood in His culture and religion. While manhood at thirteen years of age was reasonable some thousands of years prior when the tradition began, in His time He was still considered a boy. Nonetheless, after the rights of passage had successfully been accomplished and bestowed upon a proud man/boy, He received a select number of meaningful gifts. The most meaningful was a gold ring given by His most loving mother. In a life and a time marked by poverty, it was more than just a gift; it was a treasure He would wear with great honor. His mother, proud she could bestow such a present on Him, and infused with those concerns mothers always seem to recognize before there is occasion to have them, had instructed Him, "Do not ever let that ring off your finger. Do not entrust it to anyone." He had heard what she advised, but only listened with half of Himself, for He had believed He did not need such guidance given His newly attained lofty status.

In the poor urban neighborhood in which He had lived, someone knew someone who knew someone who knew someone else, and word spread about the boy who believed He was a man and sported a valuable gold ring.

The devious among them set up a deliberate accidental meeting with the boy at the local pharmacy wherein all matters of business and communication occurred. When the boy happened along, the con man had innocently asked if He would deliver a package to a nearby address for him. This had not been an uncommon occurrence in that environment. Boys who frequented the pharmacy could earn a few pennies if they would run an errand for the locals. Because the pharmacy housed one of the very few telephones in the neighborhood, boys would run to fetch the individual for whom a call was received. Likewise, they would deliver a prescription from the pharmacy or a purchase from a local shop.

And so it was that the setup began. He had eagerly agreed to deliver the package for the man who projected a false insecurity of deceit onto the boy by asking, "How do I know you are honest? What assurance do I have that you will not run off with my package and not return?"

The man/boy who was at that moment just a boy had regaled the wily con man with assurances of his honesty. To this, the con man had responded, "Give me something that will show your good faith and help me trust you."

"But what can I give you?" the boy had asked. "I have given you my word."

As if noticing it for the first time, the man had looked down at the boy's hand and said, "Give me your ring. I will hold it as collateral and return it after you have delivered my package and come back. And, I will give you ten cents for this job as it is very important."

The boy knew good fortune when it crossed His path. Ten cents was a fortune! He ignored the nagging cautions from His mother that threatened to derail this wonderful opportunity and slipped the testimonial to His recently earned manhood from his finger and handed it to the villain. Knowing (while trying not to know) that He was taking a great chance, the boy ran off with the package, traveling as fast as his young legs would carry Him.

When He arrived at the stated address, there was nothing but an empty lot. In an instant, dread was stirred into a ferocious mixture of remorse, shame, humiliation, and the relinquishing of a manhood so briefly held. You already know the outcome. He returned to the pharmacy to find the man and his ring gone, never to be seen again.

You can fathom the combination of fear and mortification that enveloped Him as He reluctantly started toward home. While most of what transpired upon the mother's and son's reunification that day has either been lost to time or deliberately repressed, what He did remember was that He was charged with the reparations for the loss of that ring little by little over the course of a year. That was the last time He succumbed to defeat without a battle. It was the last time He would allow Himself to experience humiliation.

So when He could no longer hold a book, and the fatigue that came too swiftly to His eyes defeated the purpose of the tray table that supported his reading material, All Who Loved Him presented Him with a series of audio courses on history and a very elaborate player, once again in an attempt to outmaneuver The Thief.

This wretched Thief that thrived on the suffering and heartache of others did not receive well the power of love and effort that continued to thwart its goals. Just as Sampson could single-handedly defeat an army, so did The Thief set about to do the same against the army of All Who Loved Him, The One He Chose, and He, Himself. The difference between them was that The Thief was not a being who lost its moral compass to be hardened and softened by the passage of time with an end goal of redefining itself in a lofty capacity, as was Sampson. The Thief was a being that thrived upon destruction, pain, and devastation, and the only growth it sought was an ever-increasing capacity to inflict more of the same.

Not to be defeated by this army weaponized simply by wisdom and love, The Thief decimated the newest conquest by stripping away the mental stamina that He still had left. As He tried to engage Himself in the stimulating and growth-enhancing historical courses, The Thief shut Him down. After a short foray into these lessons, He could no longer maintain his focus or concentration, and with great sorrow and disappointment, had to accept defeat, once again.

Chapter 21
Persimmons

*"I'm not special. I'm not unique.
I'm just another banana on the bunch."*

There was little He could now do for Himself without the help of The One He Chose. All matters of hygiene and self-care were no longer under His control. Eating had become quite the challenge as His food required the delicate preparation of being presented in child-sized bites in order to be chewed and swallowed.

However, memory did not fail Him as He reminisced about his lifelong eating prowess, which had reliably consumed nearly inhuman quantities of food. He floundered in his own yearning to accommodate the voracious appetite for not only nutrition but also for pleasure (as He used to do), and contrasted that with the tiny unfulfilling bites of the present. The unsteadiness of His hands eliminated the possibility of navigating food from plate to mouth without having most of it spill into areas that were of no use for feeding—even when He was presented with a state-of-the-art, ergonomic utensil created explicitly for the purpose of compensating for such a challenge. No longer was He able to swill half a glass of soda in one swallow. His liquids had to be thickened to prevent choking or aspirating, leaving no such option as imbibing an ordinary beverage. Now, He, who had been a man of a voracious appetite, required high-caloric supplement beverages to ensure He had the required complement of nutrients to maintain His weight.

The simple pleasures of filling His days with social activities such as playing cards with friends, having an afternoon at the pool, strolling through a mall or local fair, or engaging with others on a plane that reflected equivalency of body, mind, and soul had now become impractical or impossible. Years earlier, when He initially made His transition from a man of labor to one who lives to enjoy its fruits, He settled into a ritual that provided Him with the opportunity to experience the gustatory pleasure that He had enjoyed throughout His life.

This enjoyment of food, and the necessity for Him to live enjoyably, had to take a prominent role in His new life. So, He and a number of newfound friends created a partnership consisting of a weekly foray to enjoy a meal together. They called themselves the ROMEOS, an acronym for "Raunchy Old Men Eating Out." Thursday afternoons called these men together for an outing in which they laughed heartily, ate heartily, and shared their maleness heartily. This was a weekly event that was sacred to the ROMEOS from the time it began before His destiny had crossed paths with The Thief. To The Thief's dismay, it continued until well after it had pillaged and plundered His being. Fortunately, The Thief's plundering of His life did not bring an end to these outings with the ROMEOS. Instead, He continued this interest now with an escort. The One He Chose accompanied Him on these forays, providing the arms and the hands that no longer could do the job of feeding. Eventually, and not because of Him or the victories of The Thief, but the succumbing of the other ROMEOS to the ravages of time, the forays came to an end.

He recalled how before The Thief began its years of ownership over His body, The One He Chose would send Him to the store to gather a few items required to prepare a meal or to entertain guests. This was not a chore for Him but an opportunity. One of His favorite activities had been strolling through a grocery store, or even more preferably, a specialty food store, to acquire parcels of exotic tastes and enticing produce and victuals. "Just follow the list," The One He Chose would implore of Him. He might as well have been instructed to walk on one foot or to cease breathing. He would set out on this excursion, imploring one or more of All Who Loved Him to join him on this incredible journey. She would often agree to accompany Him simply because His excitement was irresistible and it was palpable as to how important it was for Him to share this experience with those He loved.

Persimmons. What fascinated Her was how He waited with hungry anticipation for the Fall season to arrive. He did not yearn for its resplendent display of color to the trees. He did not eagerly await the cool crispness in the air that was not cold enough to bring a chill but did dispense with the blistering heat of the summer. He impatiently, longingly, looked forward to the fall for its arrival of persimmons in the grocery store's produce section. A display of ripe, plump specimens, showing off the juicy and delectable flavor they harbored inside, was enough to make His head spin and His mouth water.

He would choose half a dozen persimmons and gently place them in His cart. He had an uncanny knack for picking out the sweetest fruit at its peak of ripeness so that the flavor not only filled one's mouth but jumped into the imagination, to be available as needed. This He accomplished simply by giving a squeeze or a sniff to the produce. He taught Her this skill. "Squeeze a cantaloupe at both ends," He would advise. "It shouldn't be too firm; it should have a little give. Now smell it. You should be able to smell the sweetness; if you can't, it's no good."

He taught Her patiently and earnestly as if picking the ripest of the ripe and the sweetest of the sweet would be a foundation for a good life. She listened and She learned, but She, watching Him, believed in Her child's mind that no mortal could ever acquire the gift that He had.

She could acknowledge that these jaunts to the grocery store were more interesting than pleasurable. Bearing witness to the acquiring of the foodstuffs that He would later engulf Himself provided some interesting background for the theater of consumption He would later present at the dinner table. As She accompanied Him around the store, She observed His increasing excitement as He acted on his ever-expanding need to possess the exciting new and different items He discovered as He moved up and down the aisles. She, meanwhile, silently thought about the reaction of The One He Chose upon seeing the arrival of a truckload of parcels she didn't request. That was how it was. The One He Chose and All Who Loved Him understood that there was no possibility in the universe that He would ever return from a food store with only one parcel.

Chapter 22
Transition

*"I learned how to speak about emotions.
I was wrong before, and I missed a lot."*

The one part of Him that The Thief could not steal was His cognition—His incredibly sharp mind was able to instantly add an endless series of numbers verbally pitched at Him without a breath of hesitation. One might wonder if retaining such cognition in this circumstance is truly a blessing as the mind is acutely aware of what the body is losing. Not many people are equipped to handle such a change, one that does not find an endpoint, but instead finds an infinity. The Thief saw to it that with each and every adaptation to its last attack, the weary still could not rest, for the subsequent attack was already in progress.

This encapsulates the story of Him. He was able to brush Himself off and steel Himself for assault after assault, not unlike His ability in the army to continue to run in the blazing sun far beyond any reasonable human endurance. The significant difference is that now He is the opposite of a strong young man with a body hardened by months of arduous training. He is, instead, a man with the same philosophy as that hardened young man, but in a body that has been relentlessly beaten and bruised beyond the point of recovery, with an adversary that had engraved in stone its mission to never, ever give up.

In concert with His nature, He accepted what must be accepted—that the loss of bodily functions was continuous and irreversible. Also in concert with His nature, He would now continue to wage His personal war on a battleground where He could muster a fair challenge.

First, He had some learning to do. While the functioning of His body had been fully explored, understood, and utilized to its maximum potential throughout the decades in which His younger self thrived, His inner self had been sectioned off into a compartment that lay so deeply inside that He had oft neglected to notice its very existence. This inner self encompassed emotional perusal, emotional expression, philosophies of life, and a spiritual connection with the universe.

This compartmentalized selfhood had its roots in His childhood. Growing up poor in a rough neighborhood on inner-city streets necessitated that those in His peer group sacrifice philosophical thinking and exploration. Survival meant that growth and development had to be action-oriented and goal-directed. To be otherwise would have been an invitation to the predators that gobbled up the weak.

So, the mind that had rarely dwelled in these foreign pastures now began to struggle with the reality of what The Thief was spawning, and this mobilized the quest for change and a different sort of engagement with life. On one ordinary day, at the inception of one anticipated casual conversation, She asked Him, "How are you feeling?" His reply, one She had not expected, indicated that He had been venturing into the depths of other-thinking that was familiar to Her but unusual for Him.

As He sat, curled forward in His wheelchair, His head effortfully straining to maintain an upright position, His hands shaking violently, and His breath being forced out in short bursts, He answered, "I can't walk, I can't see, I can't hear, I can't feed myself, I can't swallow. I can only speak with difficulty. I can't take care of myself."

Knowing She had to draw from whatever wisdom She could access, She took Her time to answer. She knew She loved Him enough to know better than to offer Him platitudes. She knew Him well enough to believe He was seeking a new pathway to find meaning in His current situation. She knew they both knew He had many more challenges ahead of Him, and that in order to fulfill His desire to continue on, He must learn how to engage with, adapt to, and accept on a profound level what was taking place.

She thought of empathizing with His suffering when it occurred to Her to first determine if He was, in truth, suffering. Isn't suffering a subjective event? If one does not feel they are suffering, even if others place that label on them, are they suffering? How does one conceptualize that? Some would say suffering is the conscious endurance of pain and distress. However, that definition disregards an individual's self-assessment. Isn't it possible to endure pain and not consider it suffering? For Him, pain was something to be tolerated and overcome. Distress was a feeling that had to be understood and accepted to the point that it no longer had the same impact. In His case, He did the work to nullify those impediments. No, He was not suffering. He was struggling. And through this understanding, She knew how to respond to Him.

She understood then that His list of losses was not really about what He had forfeited. His list was the opening statement to a discussion on the meaning of life. After He lamented all that He had lost, She asked Him, "How does that make you feel?"

His response, "Why is this happening to me?" confirmed for Her what it was He really wanted to explore. He needed to understand it in order to embark on acceptance. He was not to be comforted with expressions of the arbitrariness of life's challenges. If He was expected to live in this condition, He must know the purpose.

This was the beginning of His transition from a man of the body to a man of the soul. This was the beginning of His transition from one who derived His pleasures in life from external experiences to one who instead found His meaning and purpose in deeper, more cerebral and spiritual ways. This was the beginning of His surrendering His body to the destruction caused by The Thief and the building of an internal self that The Thief could never access. This was the beginning of His transition to a more exalted self. And that was a good thing.

The Thief observed the evolution of self that was taking place and thus its determination to break Him multiplied. This time, having had less-than-satisfying victories knocking Him about, The Thief concocted a new plan of attack. The twisted grin on the face of evil reflected the win it thought it had. In truth, it came alarmingly close to overwhelming His resolve and putting an end to the war between them.

The Thief weaponized itself with bacterial infections, MRSA, and sepsis in a triple-pronged attack that resulted in the destruction of bodily functions, requiring the permanent implantation of catheters. When the battle was over and He survived what for any other mortal would have been fatal, She asked Him how He was. She knew not what to expect, recalling the very nascent beginnings of the transition He was about to embark upon before this latest assault. He answered Her with the honesty they both wanted. "These two weeks have been very rough," He told her. "I thought it was the end. I was so weak I could not move. In fact, I couldn't do anything."

She asked Him in the direct way through which She had become comfortable speaking with Him, the only purpose of which was to ensure He did not have to carry any burdens alone, "Were you afraid?"

He answered, "No, I was not afraid; when you can't eat, you can't walk, you can't breathe, you can't talk, your whole body fails you, and you can't do anything, you just want to go already, but I didn't let go because I didn't want to hurt you girls and your mother."

She needed to tell Him that it was okay to let go. She said, "When you are ready to go, we will take care of each other. You can be whole and not have to suffer anymore."

His answer, so simple but yet so comprehensive was, "I'm glad. I'm feeling better now." She knew what He was telling Her, and He knew She understood this.

She told Him She loved Him. He told Her, He loved Her and they said good night. And She wept. She wept until Her eyes were swollen and She thought Her heart would break. She wept with sadness for the immeasurable burdens He carried. She wept for His struggle, the agony of His consideration of other versus self. Most of all, She wept even more from the impact of His selflessness. He chooses to go on, accepting whatever wretchedness The Thief would impose upon Him, in order to give All Who Loved Him a little more of Himself. In the end, whatever The Thief took, it could not have the essence of Him, all that was truly His, and His love for The One He Chose, for All Who Loved Him, and for All Of Those He Loved. Perhaps it was because of what The Thief took from Him that He came to understand this.

Chapter 23
Introspection

*"If there's a fire, you put water on it.
You change what you can. It'll work if you believe."*

As He ventured forth on His transition, He and She found a cache of perspectives He was ready to explore. They embarked on the notion of suffering. As noted, She had already done a great deal of exploration into this concept, but now the time had come for them to explore it together. As She had already deduced, He did not consider Himself a victim. She opened the conversation by asking Him, "How do you conceptualize what you are experiencing?"

With a mind profound in its explorations and evidencing extensive cogitation, He replied, "I don't feel it's unjust; I don't feel as if I have been chosen to suffer." He added, "A lot of people suffer." She was relieved to hear Him affirm this perspective further. "People are not given these diseases because they are bad or evil. It's the luck of the draw. I do not feel despair."

He continued, clearly following the trajectory of His mental journey. "I did feel more positive when I thought I could improve." She recalled the horrible fall He took a few years prior, one that shattered both His shoulder and His leg. Had He been doing anything daring or even remotely risky, one might be better equipped to rationalize such an outcome, but all He had done was stand up with support in order to move from chair to wheelchair. "After that, I became sad and depressed, but I saw how my wife and my children rallied to support me, and that helped a lot."

A result of that turn of events was a magnified disability that impeded what little functioning He'd still had. He knew that a whole new set of adjustments, not just to body but to mind, were necessary. Always seeking the kernel of positive, even in the most painful and challenging of circumstances, He continued, illustrating how He moved in tandem with the unfolding limitations. "I try to be as small a nuisance as I can be," He explained. "I try to make my life as livable as I can, and I try to cope as best as I can."

His efforts to explore the solutions to what adaptations were required resided in what He had already resolved, and He used those solutions to explain not just to Her, but to Himself. "Years ago, when I tried to walk and my legs turned to rubber, I knew it was time to give up my driver's license. I would not try to drive and risk hurting someone."

> "It was when I worked for Him that I got my education despite having gone to college and law school. He was the best professor I ever had. Throughout hours of talking He taught me about everything: business, Wall Street, politics, history, current events, and His favorite topic, His family. He had amazing insight, and He taught me how to fight my fears and to fight for what I wanted." —J.B.

She reflected on the infinite experiences She had encountered in which elderly people fought bitterly over surrendering their licenses. The pain of such an undertaking lay in the representation of a significant loss of independence that fundamentally marked a deterioration of functioning that would eventually result in the helplessness so characteristic of the fragility of old age. She could not help but consider how the great majority of people in such a quandary can only focus on their own losses; they are unable to ascertain the objective danger to others by continuing an activity in which they are no longer competent. In contrast, He seemed always to be motivated to shuffle together the pros and cons, the hurts and the benefits, such that His decision was stamped with what was morally responsible.

His reflection on His own forfeiture of this hallmark of independence reminded Her of the dilemma He had faced decades earlier when He found Himself in a situation that would not have ruffled a lesser man but had forced Him into a decision that would cause Him years of angst. "Light duty," a result of the injuries sustained in His childhood accident, was His assignment in the army. As a classification specialist, He was charged with pairing the new recruits with the positions that best suited them. He interviewed the fresh-faced young men. He administered the tests. He had the job of giving them their assignments. It was simple and straightforward until it was not…until one young man told Him his story.

In his local neighborhood, this young man, barely more than a boy, had been approached by a sergeant whose purpose it was to convince the naive to enlist in the army. "I WANT YOU FOR U.S. ARMY" with a picture of patriotic Uncle Sam pointing your way, was the poster tacked up on every street corner and every billboard. Whatever it took, promises that one had neither the right nor the authority to give, were dispensed like candy with nary a shred of conscience in the quest to secure the servitude of each recruit. The young man fell into the clutches of the dishonorable opportunist when he, a passionate and talented musician and a skilled instrumentalist, was guaranteed placement in the U.S. Army Band. Excited that He could serve his country while indulging in his passion and avoiding the risk of losing life or limb, the young man eagerly consigned his name and his freedom to the other.

When the day arrived that this young man ventured into His office, eagerly awaiting his assignment in the Army Band, he shared the story of the promise of the sergeant and his enlistment. He, sympathetic to the young man's situation, was forced, nonetheless, to explain that the U.S. Army Band had no openings for him. In truth, the young man's test scores did not meet the criteria to be admitted into the Army as a musician. The devastated young man burst into tears, a tidal wave of emotions washing over him. Disappointment surfaced first, followed by a sense of betrayal, then finishing with terror as He realized his enlistment was confirmed, but He would be placed in the infantry.

For Him, an injustice was an injustice and a just man had an obligation to right a wrong. He felt sorrow for the wreck of the man sobbing before Him with his boyhood in the rearview mirror of his life. He was compelled to restore the honor of the U.S. Army that was disgraced by an opportunistic sergeant. He did not fail to consider that He also bore the weight of the rules that dictated the assignments He made, and the responsibility therein. Pulled in opposing directions like an over-stretched piece of taffy and additionally hampered by a minimal parcel of time in which to sort through a quandary of Solomonic proportions that was rooted in His principles, He had to make a split-second decision, and He did just that.

Asking the desolate young man to wait for Him, He retreated into a private room, and with the stroke of a pencil, the sorry soul now had a score that beckoned an invitation into the U.S. Army Band in Washington, D.C. The destiny was sealed with a sworn promise between two men, whose paths had been brought together by powers unknown, to never utter a word about the fate of one that was forever changed by the other in the little private office on that notable day. Tears of despair changed to tears of gratitude as the indebted young man practically worshipped the empathetic soul who saved him, and he promised with his whole being he would never, ever tell a soul about what had transpired.

Insomnia was His nightly companion for months following the passage of seven days, whereupon He received a letter from the even more enthusiastically grateful mother of the young man who had sworn to eternal secrecy, thanking Him for what He did for her son. The mother bestowed upon Him all of the blessings within her reach, searching backward into the blessings of the patriarchs of her faith and praying for His long life. One would fancy He would bloat with the gratitude of the mother of a son given safe harbor in the midst of a deadly storm, but happiness was the antithesis of what He experienced as He realized the secret gift was not a secret at all. Frantically tearing up the letter and flushing it down the toilet until not a trace of it remained, in a state somewhere between panic and hysteria that His deed be discovered, He glumly reflected on His own fate should His actions be discovered. "Why did I do this?" Over seventy years later, as He recounted that amazing, yet dreadful day, He laughed as He recalled when terror nearly separated Him from His own morality.

And so, in reviewing the choices He had made in life, some that in a convoluted way appeared to have been to His own detriment at the time, He was too humble to admit that they actually elevated Him as a human being. He continued examining and explaining, trying His best to convey the newly emerging philosophies He was building that had their roots in who He had always been.

Then and now, He was one who strove toward acceptance of what life placed in front of Him. He used what wisdom, power, and impulse He had in a quest to find the optimal path to travel. He reviewed and weighed His choices. Just as He had done a lifetime earlier for the young recruit, He weighed His choices regarding how He would navigate His life as it was under attack by The Thief. He decided, "I am not going to wring my hands or cry or curse my fate. It is what it is." In fact, He found His faith deepening, creating an even greater affinity with a higher power. He understood that He was living His destiny, and while He may not know the totality of the reasons why this particular destiny was His, His faith dictated that it was meant to be.

He shared with Her that as His struggles deepened and He worked to keep suffering at bay, He became more sensitive to other people's feelings. He believed His challenges had made Him a better person, which synergistically enabled Him to be more attuned to His faith. This man, who was once a boy growing up on the urban streets of the inner city, who functioned in accordance with the practical, was now a philosopher in deep contemplation of profound meaning.

Understanding how He was processing the ceaseless deterioration of His body and His ability to function was of utmost importance to Her. While there was a large difference between the deterioration He was undergoing and what others experience as merely a function of normal aging, there is still some small degree of comparison. Therefore, there is content with which any individual can derive valuable information by hearing Him describe His own process. He summarized by explaining, "I am ninety-seven years old, and ninety percent of my friends are dead.

Life is desirable, and I still have mine."

He went further. "They don't just hand out ninety-seven. I am living, and that is good." If one believes in such things, perhaps the prayers seventy-six years prior of the mother of that young soldier had something to do with that.

So, He never taught Her how to throw a ball or mend a broken heart, but He did teach Her how to live, not just by being alive, but by embracing what you can and accepting what you cannot.

Chapter 24
Success

*"Whether you aggravate or not,
some things are not going to change."*

"The men had to put their arms around me to help me get out of the car. Then, two men came over and put their hands under my arms and helped me walk into the store." He suffered terribly from the nearly unbearable agonies of sciatica. This He did acknowledge was suffering. He was a relatively young man in the throes of early midlife in an era when a man was defined by the sort of provider He was. The typical man of that era sported pride from carrying such an ethos, but there were those who held this standard with a much more stringent regard than others. For Him, it was the highest degree by which He set His personal standard. This does not imply that His standard was extreme wealth or power. His standard was a function of what The One He Chose and All Who Loved Him desired.

"They placed me in a chair behind the register and that

is where I sat all day," He recalled. She, recalling the bizarre contraption they called "traction" that had been erected in His bedroom at the time, asked why He never took some more time off. Why He would not forgo two forty-five minute commutes that sandwiched a twelve-hour workday in an attempt to heal?

"I would not stay home and lose my trade," He said. But that one time, He did. Her young incredulous eyes were begging for explanations as to why He was lying in bed with pulleys suspending His leg in the air. Even at that tender age She had an awareness that the situation must be very serious if He was not going to work. He did not feel pain. He did not get sick. He did not succumb. So, what was this about? Perhaps this was the moment in Her young life when the beginning of the reality that He was not indestructible was instilled, only to be quickly repressed as He and She decided that was not the man He chose to be.

Several days and even more nights of this ancient remedy did little to rectify the injurious juxtaposition of vertebrae and cartilage but did accomplish enough to allow for a return to work and reinstatement of Himself as defined by His own ethos.

Decades later, when He and She reflected on those arduous times, He explained, "In those days, the dollar was hard to obtain. It was very difficult for a man to earn a living and support his family. In the busy seasons, I opened the store at 9:00 in the morning and closed up at 10:00 p.m. I sold all I could sell."

He shared with Her the origins of this multigenerational work ethic as He told of His own father, a poor immigrant coming to this country at twelve years of age, not schooled in the English language, and armed with only a fifth-grade education. The importance of having pennies to feed the bellies of hungry children transcended the importance of learning in any formal manner. Days were spent by His father peddling sandwiches that were made by His father's mother. When He was little more than a boy, He went to work in someone's shop. Long hours, laborious days of serving others, learning a language and a culture day after day, month after month, year after year eventually earned His father the privilege of opening his own shop. It was this shop that beckoned to Him for His devotion so many years later when His back begged Him for a reprieve.

And so, this legacy given to Him by His father, whose last words to Him before he took his final breath were "take care of the store," was to work hard, provide well, and know that that is what defines you as a respectable man. She recalled those long days when She had barely time to see Him—days when He left home early in the morning and returned at bedtime. "My time spent working did not upset me because I worked to make my wife and my children happy. I literally broke my back to support my family," He confided. "When your siblings and you wanted something, I did what I could to provide it. Eventually, my back got somewhat better. There was always pain, but that was the way it was."

As She sat with Him, She asked why He had never shared these feelings before. She had known the pain He suffered from sciatica—not because He spoke of it, but because of His awkward stance, which served to provide minimal relief from the nerve fibers sending shockwaves from His back down through His buttocks and into His leg.

His answer, so reflective of His humble nature, was, "I didn't share my feelings because it would have felt like boasting." He was not a martyr. He did what He believed a man should do. He worked as hard as He believed a man should work. He bore up under distress, be it the pain of sciatica or interminably long workdays, six days a week, because that was what He was taught and that was what He accepted as right. In His mind, He did nothing special. His choices were not notable. He was just an ordinary man doing what ordinary men do.

She, on the other hand, knew He was no ordinary

> "I've always known my grandfather to be a strong, loyal, levelheaded man of integrity. He was a hard-working guy who kept His emotions close to the vest. My favorite thing about Him is how He was willing to grow and learn so that later in life He was able to show the emotions others needed." —A.G.

man, and life had taught Her that it was a very special man who conducted Himself with such dedication, grace, and humility—and She told Him so. He replied to Her reflection, "I am well paid with your acknowledgment that I succeeded. I know I succeeded because you are someone I am proud of." That is who He is, one who will grab the mirror of reflection so that any compliment is instantly cast back onto the giver.

After more than half a century of working and providing for one's family, how does one judge their own success? Is it measured by the wealth accumulated? Is it assessed by the contentment of loved ones? Is success judged by how many jobs one has created or how many donations one has made to charitable causes? Perhaps all of these factors weigh into the final judgment, but for Him it was quite simple. He felt confident He succeeded as a provider and a father simply because She saw Him as such, and simply because She was someone He was proud of.

Chapter 25
New Old Man

*"My mother came to me in a dream
and said I'd live to be 105.
What would you like to do between now and then?
Breathe!"*

How does one adapt to the shift from a lifetime of being an independent, proud, self-sufficient man who is inclined to lead others, not by choice but simply by His presence, to one who, for all intents and purposes, is helpless; one who needs assistance with the most arduous to the simplest of tasks? How does one manage to go from a man who once was riveting in his hearty zeal for consuming a daily meal to one who must wear a bib while being fed by another as He gags? How does a man who was once able to drink a half glass of soda in a single swig cope with being able to quench His thirst using only artificially thickened beverages imbibed in small sips in order to prevent aspiration?

How does one adjust to the transformation of a tall,

handsome, well-postured man whose stride was confident and powerful, to one who is so frail and devoid of muscle as to make His bones visible beneath the skin; one who bruises, tears, and bleeds with the slightest provocation; one whose skeleton bent nearly in half or folded over in a wheelchair, requiring a strenuous effort to keep His head momentarily upright? This man-of-the-body-no-more now lived behind shuttered eyes, the lids of which had become so heavy the effort to open them was less rewarding than living in darkness.

You would think such a man would retreat to the safety and privacy of His shelter, a place in which pride would not be challenged by the observations, judgments, or pity of others. This was not the case. He confronted this challenge as He had always confronted challenges. While His legs could no longer stand, He stood up in the face of all The Thief had taken, and He carried on with some minor and some major adjustments in a way similar to the one in which He had carried on before. He had continued His weekly outings with the ROMEOS, ironically outliving them all, until each one of them took their final bow. He accomplished this by taking along The One He Chose to feed Him while the others ate as men ate. The One He Chose fed Him, she wiped Him, she cleaned the food that had escaped His mouth and made its way down his shirt, and then she retired to a separate table with her own company while He embraced the opportunity to be a proud man in all manners available to Him…and He enjoyed Himself.

One might wonder how he was able to persevere. The answer lies in who He always knew Himself to be. Internally, He was still Him. He was not simply an old, sick man. He was a culmination of every age, every experience, and every man He ever was. Within Him existed not only the present self but also the infinite number of past selves, and this allowed Him to be whoever He needed to be in any given moment.

So, in a peaceful moment, long after the ROMEOS had either passed on or scattered to the places old people go, He and She shared thoughts and memories of experiences from long ago. This took place at a time when laughter was hard to come by as the weight of His situation bore down heavily. She was reading to Him Her notes of times past, and He began to chuckle. Before long, they were laughing as He reminded Her, "I remember the time when you wanted to kill me!"

Although He was legitimately an old man now, He had always been old in a sense, even when young. Most would probably refer to this trait as "old fashioned."

He said to Her, "I remember when your mother and

I were supposed to be away overnight but instead came home. I thought there was a burglar in the house when I drove up and saw the lights on. I walked in and found you with your fiance planning a far-too-romantic evening together. No daughter of mine was going to do that before She was married!"

She laughed as She recalled the fury She felt as her evening of romance with her betrothed had been spoiled. She concurred, "Yes, I do think I was about to kill you, especially since we both knew you were a total hypocrite! I recall the exploits you have shared with me about broken-hearted girls you left in your wake as, shall we say, a rather adventurous young man." And they laughed at the ridiculous nature of what was and what had not really mattered after all.

What was not overtly addressed between them, but they were both thinking, was the reality of how, as we journey through life, our priorities become rearranged. He, as a young man, was focused on the conquest of female affections. He had been proud enough of His historical successes to revel with Her in the accountings of being caught in questionable situations with some man's daughter or attempted seductions by another man's wife. What had been entertaining and humorous as a young man became horrifying when a comparable situation arose between His own daughter and a young man. And now, many decades later, when that young man had long since made, as He would define it, "an honest woman of Her" and had sired their children, grandchildren, and great-grandchildren, that night long, long ago when He surprised the young couple mattered not in the slightest.

And as they reminisced and laughed, She could almost reach out and touch the man that was His younger self. She caught a mental whiff of the clean pleasant scent of Him, the man who was fastidious about His hygiene, whose fragrance revealed a mixture of soap and aftershave. He would never present with a shirt untucked or a shoe worn with scuff marks, as His regimen of polishing his leather shoes was undertaken with regularity using the "state-of-the-art" electric buffer that now had been obsolete for generations.

She could not unsee the comparison between the man He was and the man He had become. She also could not help but admire the grace with which He initially fought, then accepted, then embraced, and then accepted even more fundamentally, all that was changing.

So, His adaptation continued even as The Thief coveted and stole what it could. He doggedly ventured to fight all He could reasonably defend. He was continually pressed to lower the bar on His own expectations of self. This allowed

Him the ability to find pride when the accomplishment was a mere whisper of what was accomplished previously. Evidence of this was that while the energetic, fast-paced athletically impressive game of paddleball was a memory of years past, He now conducted His exercises from His bed.

He proudly reveled in the successes of His current exercises. He told Her, "I do arm raises; I raise my hands up…and down…up and down. When I'm feeling strong, I use my weights—sometimes one pound, sometimes I can lift two pounds." He shared with Her, "I also do my scissor kicks. I push my legs together and then apart." He was as pleased with Himself as He was when He had traveled eight miles on His stationary bicycle going nowhere.

She understood that He was telling Her that transitions, even transitions that are drastic and to others may appear insurmountable, can be managed when you shift the criteria by which you define yourself. The once strong young man had a criteria for strength that was in concert with His age and fitness. The current sick old man had simply adopted new criteria that was reasonable for His situation, hence making Him a new man who was aged as opposed to an old man. Living up to such criteria allowed Him to feel proud and adaptable, and that is exactly what He was.

Chapter 26
Reflection

"I'm not afraid of what's happening. I know I need to die. I just don't need to rush."

She knew She had to read Her story of His life to Him before She could share it with others. She wrote, She read, He listened, He commented, they laughed, they reminisced, and together they sewed together bits of Him from yesteryear, weaving the fabric of who He had been with who He was continuing to become.

What simultaneously astounded and bewildered Him was how He was perceived through the eyes of Her younger self. When She completed reading to Him the chapter, "The Ice Cream Soda," He was silent for a while. "Dad?" She was sure He had fallen asleep. Miffed at how He could sleep while she related the pearls of His life, She asked, "Dad, are you awake?" A moment more passed before He spoke.

"What's so important about an ice cream soda?" He

asked. "The gist of an event is more important than the facts of an event. An event happens, and at the time you think of it as an ordinary occurrence of the day, but over time it becomes a moment that is golden. I didn't realize it but it was an event of love."

He continued, "The father and His daughter were together in a family that loved one other." He recognized for the first time that a humorous impulse to entertain All Who Loved Him with a silly story about a cherished dessert many decades past became a defining event for Her.

"The story wasn't forgotten. The memories have lingered on, and you have thought enough of my story to memorialize it," He said.

She responded, "Dad, it was so much more than an entertaining story; there were so many lessons embedded in it. You embodied the man that You were and conveyed the values that were so important to teach Your children. You told the story of a man who would go to great lengths to help a stranger in trouble. You told the story of that stranger's relief at being helped out of a deeply troubling, life-threatening situation, and the gratitude He both felt and expressed for that help."

Without planning or noticing it, He had told the story of Himself, His values, and the sort of person He admired and strove to be. He also told the story of how He wanted his children to be. "I told you a story that shows every human being has value," He stated simply.

As they continued to share this memory, He realized He hadn't thought of the story of the ice cream soda and the Indian Chief in a long time. What had been created in a spontaneous moment of affection for both the enjoyable confection and All Who Loved Him had become a pathway to a collection of memories, those of standing around the kitchen table with a bevy of salivating youngsters ready to jump at His every command. "You get the seltzer," He would order, and therein was produced the not yet ancient, but very ordinary for the time, blue glass jar of seltzer with the metal finger pump that carbonated the water. Then, "You get the syrup," meant Fox's U-Bet, the only chocolate syrup worthy of blending with the ingredients of this splendid beverage.

"You get the ice cream," came next, followed by whatever else He requested that will remain confidential in deference to the esteemed chief—all to allow for the mixing and combining of ingredients for the world's most secret and delicious ice cream soda.

As He listened to Her recounting of His ancient tale, He commented, "It's a sweet memory of a time and a place that would have been lost forever, a time of pleasures, love, disappointments, and all that life presented back then."

She now knew that He was understanding that His life had a meaning and a purpose not yet fully realized—at least not in the concrete way that words convey. She knew that She was sharing with Him His legacy, created by Him but understood and remembered by Her. She was punctuating the essay of His life of which He hadn't been aware He had spent decades writing. So, when He said, "These stories mean very little to strangers, but touch on a button in the relationship of families; they tell of the growing up of a daughter with her father; they tell of the remembering of events that at the time seemed insignificant but have grown in significance as time passed because they tell about the importance of relationships," She knew they both understood what the other was thinking. They felt the bond between them grow ever more strands, strengthening and deepening.

This guided Him even more deeply into the pondering of the purpose of a life lived. "Who will visit my grave?" He asked. "Initially people will come—my children and my grandchildren, and then no one will come anymore. I won't blame them; I understand life is busy and there will be other things you'll have to do, but eventually, no one will come." She understood His fear was that He'd be forgotten about after His death, which is tantamount to an annihilation of self and the meaning of His life. It hurt Her that He would be lost in consideration of His own meaninglessness when He was, in fact, the antithesis of that.

"Dad, do you recall telling me how my devotion to my children was reminiscent of how your mother was devoted to her own children?" She asked him. "Her devotion was instilled in you, which you instilled in me, and I, in turn, instilled those values in my own children. Even though no one visits your mother's grave, the essence of her resonates through the generations. She lives on in you, me, and my children, even though my children never knew her."

She comforted Him, explaining, "You will never be forgotten because your essence, your morals, YOU will echo through the generations. That is how you have made an impact in the world." She explained how this moves in multiple directions through the influence He had on Her, who in turn influenced Her relationships with Her spouse, Her friends, and all of those She brushed against in life. "Each person creates a ripple that moves out in wider and wider circles, ad infinitum."

Tears running down His cheeks, He answered, "I want to believe you, but I don't know what will happen when I'm dead."

"Dad, our connection is so strong and we love each other so much that that will transcend your earthly life," She assured Him. "We will find each other after you are dead; I don't know exactly how, but I know we will."

"Please, can you wipe my eyes, they're tearing. I'm feeling very emotional." So, She wiped His eyes and kissed His cheek. There was a silent agreement that His life's value surpassed the ordinary days one spends walking the earth by creating a legacy through His actions, His ethics, and His stories that would become a moral roadmap for His children and their children.

Chapter 27
Finding the "After"

"The worst part of dying is leaving my loved ones."

As time passed and His struggles invited suffering, His suffering was without end, and His recoveries were brief, followed by a worsening of His condition. He spoke to Her regularly. By now He and She both knew that such conversations could be had only between the two of them, and they were comfortable with the discussions. She asked, "How are you feeling?" He answered that He was having a better day than the one prior. She asked, "What happened yesterday?"

He answered, "I was very weak. The last two weeks were very bad."

"Bad? How?" She asked. It was unusual for Him to be so forthright about His hardships.

"I was so weak I couldn't have lifted a piece of paper if I tried. I couldn't sleep, couldn't do anything." She just listened, silently offering Him the opportunity to unburden Himself. "I thought it was the end, but I guess it wasn't because here I am, feeling better. The doctors say that's how it goes; they don't know why I have some terrible days, but then it recedes, and I feel better. I feel good now. I am grateful for what I have."

She pressed, "Tell me more." And He, knowing what She was really asking, accepted the invitation to share those reflections that He had worked and reworked privately in his consciousness over the span of weeks. He opened the gates of his newly explored pontifications and He summoned Her in—not with a physical gesture, but with the like-mindedness that they now shared.

Once She had ventured into the inner chamber of His reflections, together they shut out all else, and He told Her: "I accept that the time is drawing near when I'll have to say goodbye. I'll live a while, yet, but I am seeing the breakdowns. I see that physically, there's very little I can do on my own. Mentally, the routine things are now a challenge."

She observed that he was shaken mightily when He confessed, "This week, I couldn't remember the names of my children."

He continued, "So, I can't give you a date, it may be six months, it may be any time." She saw the shift in Him. She heard the shift in Him. She embraced the shift from one who fought to go on for another day, another hour, and another minute, to one who no longer wished to count the minutes and hunger for more. She recognized that there was a powerful and very significant transition from the countless conversations they had shared in which He, with not just sadness but confusion of sorts, listed and enumerated all that The Thief had taken from Him. Now He was moving in tandem with these losses, as opposed to standing in defiant opposition to what was unfolding.

And She, reflecting on His lengthy struggle against succumbing to the inevitable, asked Him, "Are you ready for this?"

His response, as always, was so clear and so perspicuous She could believe nothing other than that He had given this the deep and meticulous thought it warranted. "Yes," was His reply. "This is the only way to avoid the monotony of spending all day in my wheelchair. I have been relegated to solitary confinement." He did not need to explain this any further. She understood that despite having The One He Chose within reach at all hours of the day and night, and an endless, yet constantly changing sea of those who are called "caregivers" but often give sans the caring, He was in quite a solitary situation. After all, these conditions can leave one with a profound aloneness, a desolation that a thousand companions cannot relieve. His mind, sharp and strong, had become utterly and profoundly separated from his body, and a mind without a body, especially in one who had been so completely of the body, will turn inward, finding an inner world to replace the one lost.

While in this inner world, He struggled to find reasons, explanations, and any sort of sense to explain the presence and the efficacy of The Thief's agenda. He continued, "Even prisoners who are jailed and in solitary confinement have more freedom than I have. It's a horrible thing that someone who is innocent, has committed no crime, and has been a good person can be given this sentence. I can no longer walk, even with help. I forget even the mundane. I sit all day and watch shows that are different, yet all the same, which gives me a pain in the ass—both figuratively and literally!"

As the reverberations from the spoken truths of His decree settled around them, the imprisoned concepts, a result of this new plateau of contemplation He had recently achieved, issued forth. With a combination of apprehension, pensiveness, and courage, He continued. "I don't know if there is an afterlife. I know that when I sleep, it is a total blank. If I cease to exist and there is nothing for me, it might not be a bad change; I won't know anything because I won't be experiencing anything."

She listened to Him with a different type of hearing—that of what He already had sorted through, as well as his processing of the latest challenges. What becomes of a person when He confronts the cessation of living in the only manner He has ever known? How is He to maneuver through the variety of often conflicting beliefs thrown at Him throughout His lifetime regarding the "after"?

The One He Chose believed, with an absolute surety that can only belong to one with an adamant defiance to dally with the uncertain, that at the end of living there is utter nothingness. This gave little comfort and more than a moderate amount of uneasiness to a man who had always believed in the existence of a higher power and an unquestionable hereafter. He was not the type to be dismissive, and in His aging, He self-accommodated an ever-increasing input of the theoretical. Therefore, He could not help but be affected by the views of The One He Chose. He was disturbed by them but had, in His immeasurable way of incorporating the unpleasantness of what His environment brought to Him, found a system by which to weave this disturbance into an acceptable format that enabled Him to reduce some distress. And so, He tentatively pondered the potentiality of the blank nothingness.

This was, however, not the endpoint of his ponderings,

but the initiation. He explored with Her the well-worn exploration of life reborn. He knew that She had such a belief, as She had shared it many times before, often on their walks that invited such theoretical explorations as well as more recently as He and She witnessed the stealth of The Thief and the resulting deterioration of His body.

He and She endeavored to pursue thoughts on the "after." She, who was certain with an absolute assuredness that there was such a state, was able to give balance to the doubts that had intruded upon Him, disrupting His comfort. Such discussions began seriously, with the soothing notions of meeting again in another dimension, reuniting with loved ones who had already made the journey, living whole and disease-free, and so on. But before long, the conversations meandered into the realm of silly. They laughed together as the ridiculous questions bandied about between them. How old will I be there? Will there be any cats? How is there enough room for everyone? It must be very crowded. How will we find each other? And while unspoken, She was sure He wondered about what sort of cuisine the afterlife provided.

While the silly is just silly, it is quite a bit more than that. The laughter only has room to exist once the angst has ebbed. She knew that as He was able to be silly with Her, He was finding some amount of comfort that all would be okay. They would be together again and forever. He would be with His parents and brothers, and eventually, The One He Chose, and more eventually, All Who Loved Him.

This understanding created a seismic shift from death representing an ending to it introducing a transition. All would not end and goodbyes would be followed by reunions. And that was good.

Chapter 28
49th Hour

"The assets we have are only loaned to us.
Eventually, we have to give them back."

While the war continued to wage on unceasingly, with some battles won but more lost, He lamented on the futility of continuing the fight. Exactly thirty days had passed since the passage of his ninety-eighth birthday, time spent primarily living but with too great a percentage of just existing. In the space of exactly thirty days, He had been hospitalized precisely four times.

The cruelty of The Thief highlighted the balance of forces—the blessed and the evil that was so characteristic of His life, especially the later years. His blessed birthday was a miracle by virtue of the fact it even took place, and it gifted Him with one of His most treasured delights.

She had asked Him what sort of cake He would most enjoy. "I would like a cake with fruit—strawberries, blueberries, raspberries, all sorts of fruit," He told her.

"Would you like a tart? A custard-filled tart with fruit on top?" She queried.

"Yes, that is exactly what I would love to have for my birthday cake."

She made certain that would be the cake He got, and that was the cake He thoroughly enjoyed, consuming an inordinate share of His own, along with a disproportionate amount of others' shares as well. He delighted in this epicurean bliss, reminiscent of days past in which He was able to consume the foods of His passions.

The yin and the yang, the glorious and the devastating, saw to it that The Thief and the man wrestled yet again. A mere few hours after the celebratory occasion, The Thief, in a state of fury that the pretense of health waxed mightily in commemoration of a miraculous accomplishment—a victory in the war between them—unleashed an arsenal of weaponry against Him.

In its cold-blooded cruelty, The Thief whispered into the forces of life surrounding the happy occasion and let them know, "He may be able to eat, but it is I who have the ultimate power." And with that, The Thief forthwith ceased all digestive processes, such that the heavenly birthday cake made its way past His mouth and esophagus but got no farther than His stomach. And herein the opposing forces came face to face once again: the exultation of celebration with the utmost misery of bodily and psychic pain foreshadowing the cessation of life.

He was rushed to the hospital. While all sorts of modern medical equipment were hastily applied in an effort to succeed in this new battle against The Thief, the only true weapon was His will to win, which was synonymous with His will to live. No fewer than forty-eight hours were required to remove the undigestible feast from His wracked body, forty-eight hours during which the only sustenance He received came through a thin plastic tube inserted into his vein. Forty-eight hours of agonizing pain due to the monstrous, yet life-saving, equipment that was snaked down through His nose, meeting its final destination in His small intestine. Forty-eight hours of having tubes inserted to provide life-sustaining fluids and others to remove life-ending blockages. Forty-eight hours during which His world was again turned upside down and inside out, and nothing made any sense. Forty-eight hours during which The Thief hijacked the rationale of His mind, enough to disorient Him but less than was required to defeat Him; and forty-eight hours during which He was completely and totally inaccessible to Her.

And then after the forty-eight hours, there was a forty-ninth hour that brought a fragile but meaningful victory once again. The crisis was past, the tentative balance restored, and He relaxed with the knowledge that The Thief had not achieved the final victory. Much had been lost, that was a certainty, and some never to be recovered, but He had won the battle.

He reclaimed His ability to digest his food, but necessary changes to his routine placed Him even further away from His beloved enjoyment of cuisine. Still, He gladly traded them for the gift of more time among the living. This most recent battle, arduously fought, utilized the love and strength of His wishes to replenish His flagging armaments. He finally received His discharge and journeyed home.

A sigh of relief rippled throughout the breasts of All Who Loved Him when they understood that this victory was one He had fought to achieve. Each one of them would have lovingly said their final goodbyes had that been His wish.

The revelation that He had not yet acquiesced to the cessation of the monotony and hardship of the life He was sentenced to live was more of a surprise to Him than to anyone else. He was never a quitter and always a fighter, and He had always been able to rise to any new challenge, regardless of how resigned He felt. And so, He rejoined The One He Chose at home, settling in to sift through the spoils of war and determine what could be salvaged.

Chapter 29
Stupidity

"There is no point in railing against fate—you can't change it.
You might as well accept it with grace.
You change what you can and accept what you can't.
This is what gives you peace."

Complacency is a dangerous state in the purview of a deadly enemy whose defeat was received with venomous wrath, the likes of which no upstanding soul can fathom. Forty-eight hours were the wicked mockery of The Thief's latest torment, and it was forty-eight hours after He began His recovery at home that The Thief found a new portal for attack.

The body offers many vulnerabilities, and The Thief was determined to exploit every single one. The cells. Not tried before, but thoroughly deadly. Poison the cells. Create toxicity so lethal that the face and neck will swell to a magnitude that closes the throat so nothing can pass. This will end the war once and for all. The plan was brilliant in its diabolical rigor, such that The One He Chose conferred with Her about withholding treatments and just making Him feel comfortable as His final days unfolded. While She felt Her heart was nearly wrenched from her body, and the tears nearly choked Her words, She knew She had to focus on His innermost wishes. She knew His Herculean strength, and She advised, "Give Him a few days. I know He will want to fight." Herein, the body and the soul united, completely and harmoniously in their shared agenda, and in tandem they fought. After a few days, He no longer required the feeding tubes, and He took back that which The Thief had taken from Him because that was what He wanted.

When tubes were once again removed, the swelling was tamed, and communication became possible, She asked and He told Her, "I have engaged in stupidity. It was like being in a boxing ring with a six-foot-tall opponent with rippling muscles. I had tattered boxing gloves and I was getting the hell beaten out of me. I tried to stand up ten times." He began to sob, the type of sobbing that initiates from deep within and desperately needs to find a portal for its release.

She heard His words, but even more so She felt His desperation. He was literally in the fight for His life and had found Himself on the precipice of losing the ability to discern the appropriate action. "Everyone cheered my opponent because He was winning—until I fell down—and then everyone started to cheer me because of my stupidity in continuing the fight."

And He stayed in that fight until He managed to regain his advantage and was satisfied He had reversed the outcome. As tears rolled down His face, He asked Her, "Please wipe my nose." As She got up to do so, feeling a momentary sense of effectiveness at being able to provide a nominal sense of comfort for Him, She was catapulted in Her mind's eye to a time many years before. She was a small child, safely enfolded in His powerful arms as He brought Her into the ocean to introduce Her to its pleasures.

She was frightened, clutching Him, knowing He would keep Her safe when a huge wave broke far too close for comfort, splashing its salty offense right up Her tiny nose. Crying, She implored Him, "I need a tissue!" He instructed Her, "Here, blow your nose in my hand." Even at that tender age, this was not a viable option for Her. That was the end of their journey into the ocean, and the beginning of His trek across the beach to obtain for Her the requested tissue.

Here, recognition of the reversal of the roles now was bittersweet. The omnipotent, protective man that once was, was no more. They both understood that. The Thief had taken so very much.

This time She heard something different than He had previously portrayed after an arduous battle triumphantly won. There was a profound sadness in Him that edged out the exultation of the triumph. A companion to the sadness was a weariness that seeped into the innermost depth of Him, displacing His historic pride. So, She asked Him about it, and without answering Her with words, He answered Her with His sobs. The whole of His despair flowed from His fatigued body, which was convulsing against the lamentation. While acquainted with His tears from their many emotional travels, this was Her first introduction to seeing a sorrow in Him that was so deep and overpowering, and She knew what He was feeling: hopeless.

The woman wants to become the child to have the parent comfort her, but the woman knows that sometimes in life there must be a reversal of roles such that the child must, even for a moment, become the parent. More than She wanted to be comforted, She wanted to comfort Him: to hold Him physically and emotionally and help Him reconnect with the person He was and had always been. So they talked and talked, and before long they were speaking His language, the language of the spirit, the language of strength.

He became reacquainted with His strength by revisiting what had always connected Him with His vitality: war. Working through the machinations of the aggressor and the defender had become ingrained in the manner in which He viewed life. This dynamic was not limited to wars that took place on the battlefield, but defined His approach to conflicts that occurred in all of life's arenas, whether they be on the urban neighborhood streets or a fight to the finish with a thief. She now understood His passion for books and movies about war. It was all about aggressors and defenders teaching him novel strategies for making one's journey through life's challenges, and learning how good triumphs over evil.

During their conversation, He slipped in a reminiscence of World War II, the period of His awakening to Himself, and the opportunity for Him to live His beliefs. Germany, the foe of the Jewish people, had calculated their destruction just as The Thief calculated His own. Contrary to their goals, the Germans "taught the Jewish people how to take a defeat and come back, and that's what I believe in."

Before long, the resurgence of all that made Him who He was had seeped back into His weary soul, and He said to Her, "We're a team—we'll fight together and be stupid together." So She returned to being the child and He the parent, and She found that He was an inspiration at a whole new level.

Chapter 30
Overview of Life

"Those people who are really great are humble."

"I thought I was going to kick off yesterday and this morning." For a man who rarely uttered any indication of pain, His description was overpowering. "I felt like my stomach was being shredded. I was in agony. I never want my daughters or anyone else's daughter to feel that kind of pain."

There was not an iota of doubt in Her mind that the pain must have been mind-bending for Him to give it such emphasis. Remnants of the ordeal that had infiltrated His digestive tract were still wreaking havoc. "One thing I never volunteered for was to be the victim. It's a no-profit experience," He told her. She had to laugh at the juxtaposition of His description of agony with His philosophy of Himself in the world, and the humor He seemed eternally able to inject into any situation.

He continued more seriously, knowing it was safe to

share with Her what was typically left unsaid, making its mark only within the confines of His own thoughts. "Until the pain went away, I wished I would go away. I'm not afraid of what's happening. I know I need to die; I just don't need to rush."

She, feeling honored that He was willing to breach His own boundaries to safeguard the experiences that made Him feel vulnerable, ventured to inquire if it was all worth what He'd suffered.

Typical of Him, He framed his answer philosophically, replying, "With all of its trials and tribulations, I'm glad I went through the ordeal of a long life. Now let's stop talking about this bad stuff and tell me something good."

With unspoken words, they both understood that life, no matter how good or bad, is an ordeal. No one gets through a meaningful life without facing some challenges, hardships, hurts, and disappointments, along with the easy and the positive. As He articulated, "You can't win the fight without getting your hands dirty."

Another less driven individual, confined endlessly day upon day to the immobility of his own body, may allow himself the luxury of drifting off into a meaningless nothingness, sacrificing none of his very limited precious energy to sorting through the purpose of existence. He was not such a man. Looking forward to a hundred years of living offers a very different perspective than looking backward at a hundred years. He understood this now.

"Man is encouraged to use the short term of his existence here on Earth to do some good before his end comes," He said. "Man devotes a lot of time to extend the length of his life, but it's inconsequential. I am among a chosen few who have lived close to one hundred years. That's a tremendous increase in the time allocated for man to live on Earth, and I am certainly grateful for it. But, when you examine man's tenure to be allowed to improve the lot of mankind, it's pitiful how little it is."

And herein She saw the emerging philosophy of the man who was simultaneously looking backward at one hundred years lived and forward at the time one can still live. What is one supposed to do with all of those years? Is the time lived best spent in the betterment of oneself? Of one's loved ones? Of mankind? Or in some other endeavor or lack thereof?

She also recognized the frustration He was feeling, that of the incomprehensible differential between seeing the eternity of one hundred years unfolding ahead of oneself and the infinite opportunities those years represent, and the hindsight of the speed of the passage of those years and the inconsequentiality of so many of them. A hundred years in front of a person is an eternity. A hundred years in the rearview mirror is an instant.

His years had given Him an opportunity to both experience and reflect upon the best and the worst of mankind. He had not only borne witness to, but had participated in the fights against the most malignant of horrors that humankind inflicted upon itself. His pain and His cynicism were reflected in His words. "I can't reconcile life when I see how people are filled with hate and kill other innocent people. I don't think it's in the fabric of human experience to make things better because of the hatred and intolerance in humans. It makes me wonder sometimes if life is a reward or a punishment."

She, on the other hand, had a different perspective. She explained to Him that She saw life as neither a reward nor a punishment, but as an opportunity for learning, growth, and the betterment of oneself, that which would hopefully result in benefitting others. "I've read so much history regarding the advance of man from the wilderness," He stated.

Clearly, the scientific advances that humanity has perfected has created a world unimaginable to a more primitive human. But is this what is important? Is this our mission? "Mankind is like a horse pulling a wagon," He continued. "There's no choice but to go on, but it's pitiful because when you look back at the supposed gains, you realize how futile the fight was because we have had no victory."

What would victory look like? Perhaps, He pondered, the victory would be "to know that man has advanced in his thinking—from hate to love. But I wonder, what happens when the next conqueror comes along? They don't have patience for too long. They always wipe the slate clean and start over again." From one who has lived through too many wars fought over too many issues undeserving of the bloodshed accompanied by the destruction of lives, it is understandable that He would have little faith that history would not continue to repeat itself over and over again.

Knowing they had exhausted this contemplation of the meaning of life, they shifted gears, perhaps in an endeavor to explore a topic that could result in a more satisfying resolution. In the like-minded way they often thought, She, who saw the family as the microcosmic representation of society on a larger scale, was pleased as He brought the musings of all of humanity down to a manageable sphere.

"Let's talk about a father and his children. It's a closer experience of the world problem—the jealousies, attempts at cures, and the disappointments from failure and the punishments that ensue." And with that, He launched into conceptualizing the years traveled and the wars fought on a more personal level. As He reviewed the lives of All Who Loved Him, He lamented, "I've seen my children aging—winning some battles and losing others." That was what life was for Him—a combination of observing, contemplating, and assessing. There were those times when He had to engage, and others in which He had to watch from the sidelines and allow the successes and failures of His children to unfold in accordance with their own lives' trajectories.

As a parent, He reveled in the joys and shouldered the sorrows. In this arena, He was able to find a more comfortable peace than on the larger-scale issues only because He knew He had infused His progeny with the best He had to offer.

"I've come to a new set of conclusions since I was exposed to how life really works," He explained. "One day you will say 'my dad really knew where the gold lies.' That's what fathers are for; life turns a fool into a wise old man."

And when He finished His narration, He bestowed upon Her His appreciation for all She embraced in hearing Him, and He said to Her, "You're a receiver, and that's important."

She thought about all He had shared and all that He was. Often She had thought of Him as a hero, not a description

He ever would have applied to Himself. So what is a hero, really? A hero, She considered, is not someone who is perfect nor is it someone who strives for perfection. That would be unreasonable because perfection does not exist. A hero is someone who uses the life given to them to learn and to grow, someone who is willing to see and own their faults in order to improve upon them in the hope of becoming a better person, and eventually be a better person to others. To be a hero is to be a guide and a role model from whom others can learn without really knowing that that is what they are.

He never taught Her how to throw a ball, play a sport, or mend a broken heart, but He taught Her not just how to be alive, but how to live, embracing the joys that you can and accepting the sorrows that you thought were intolerable. And so, She concluded, He was, inarguably, a hero.

Chapter 31
Ending

"Nobody owes me anything.
I'm dying and can say I've had a glorious life."

She knew it was time. Year upon year of challenges had not impacted His desire to live. Death was the enemy, sometimes feared but always fought. This time it was different. Death had now become the friend; the welcoming embrace that would terminate His struggles—His suffering and the exhausting battles that He had fought every moment, every hour, every endless day, as The Thief notched its victories with increasing momentum.

The nighttime psychosis was unbearable. Nights were filled with unimaginable terrors of irrationality coupled with utter helplessness. He called for people to help Him while The One He Chose stood right by His side. Nothing could calm the ferocity of the irrational mind pickled with disease and twisted with mounting sleep deprivation.

Upon the rising sun, rationale returned but that did

little for the depleted and exhausted psyche and body. Even when one is postured to jump a hurdle, or a series of hurdles, they must have a break in between or they will catapult into disaster, and this was what was unfolding in Him. When the fateful afternoon arrived after a series of such unbearable nights, The One He Chose asked Him the simplest of questions: "What would you like for supper?" He opened His mouth to answer, mind sharp, decision made, but no words issued forth. He tried again and again, and eventually garbled words tumbled out in an unintelligible fashion. The One He Chose made the emergency call, followed by one to Her. She spoke to Him and He spoke not to Her. Gibberish. He tried but could not make Himself understood.

The passing of a few hours was all that was required to recover his speech—one of the last remaining functions The Thief had not yet conquered, but the impact had cut deeply and remained intact.

She spoke with Him on the phone as He lay in a hospital bed. He told Her, "I signed a DNR. I don't want to live like this. I don't want to live in pain. I don't want to suffer." And She knew He was done fighting.

How does one help her father die? She tried to lighten the moment. "Dad, will you do a favor for me?"

"I'll try," He answered. "What is it?"

She asked, "Will you wait a week so I can come and see you before you die?" What shattered Her was hearing the response from a man whose entire adult existence was driven by love and sacrifice

"No, a week is too long for me to suffer. If I'm in pain, it's too long."

The air between them changed and She saw, not with Her eyes, but with Her heart the tiniest gesture of invitation. His mortal enemy, whom He had ferociously battled for over a decade, the sworn enemy against whom He had mobilized every strength, every intelligence, every philosophy, and every tactic was now being invited in to take what it desired. The fight was over. He laid His armaments down, exhausted and depleted. The Thief, surprised and arrogant, sneered its twisted grin, but in its foolishness neglected to notice that no defeat had been achieved. You see, He had won. While The Thief and He battled for the functionality of His body, a much more important event was evolving. Initially, even He did not notice it. It was subtle and confusing, but as He and She spoke, it not only became apparent, but was supported and enhanced.

You see, while The Thief took everything His body had

to give, He was learning about what was really important to Him. The Thief had forced His transition from being a man of the body to being a man of the soul. That precious soul grew. It deepened and it perfected itself as His consciousness was forced into introspection once the physical self was removed. The greatest gift one can receive, that of the meaning of life, was slowly revealed to Him.

This was His meaning: to love—not just to give love, but to receive it, for letting others love you is just another way of loving them.

His meaning was to care for those He held dear, and not just by providing tangible goods, but by sharing His passions, His humor, and His wisdom.

He learned that the meaning of life is letting others see not just His strengths but His flaws, for both offer valuable opportunities for growth. It's letting Himself be vulnerable, finding the balance in pride, and being resilient, yet flexible so that arrogance is forfeited in order to be humble. He learned that living with humility enhances the spirits of all who surround Him.

His meaning was one of sacrifice, even if that meant living with pain and suffering in order to be present a little longer in the lives of those who needed Him. Perhaps most important, His meaning was to learn the lessons of life and to share them with those who would welcome the wisdom that was acquired through such an arduous and prolonged journey.

The one enormous hurdle that stood in His way was how to say goodbye. Although life held minimal joy and an inordinate amount of suffering, all of His being was wrapped around those He loved. Tearing Himself away from them required indescribable strength and insurmountable resolve, attributes that had always been defining characteristics of His, but in this situation abandoned Him completely. His love for life, second only to His love for His family, was what kept Him going for nearly ten decades. Embracing a separation from both was a struggle that was nearly all He could bear. Only His newfound belief that there would be a time and a place to be reunited allowed Him to take His leave.

She knew He had made His peace, and He was ready to close the book on His life. Whether the primary emotion was sadness or relief, She could not decipher. She was simultaneously elated that He was able to embrace letting go of His earthly life to move forward toward a place where suffering was not His constant companion, but there was still so much She wanted to learn from Him and share with Him.

She told Him, "You don't have to wait for me to get

there, but remember every moment how much I love you and that you've been an incredible father."

He responded, "I love you, too," and they said goodbye. She knew this was not the end but the beginning of the end. He had divested Himself of His weapons and tools. He had chosen to cease fighting. He was tired and knew He had achieved all of the small triumphs He was going to win. And He knew that what was left in the wake of The Thief's pillaging and plundering was the greatest gift of all. Most important was that He looked forward to being at peace. She had never seen this side of Him, and perhaps He had just given Her His final lesson.

Not The End

About the Author

Deborah Wagner, Ph.D. is a developmental psychologist who has spent the past three decades in clinical practice working with individuals of all ages, as well as couples and families. She is the author of The Fifth Decade, *Is It Just My Life or Is It Perimenopause?*, which was inspired by her work with perimenopausal women and their families. Dr. Wagner has dedicated her career to understanding and helping patients navigate lifespan development and its impact on human emotions, reactions, and psychology. With her patients, she focuses on optimizing how they live so that they can lead better, more successful lives.

www.ingramcontent.com/pod-product-compliance
Lightning Source LLC
Chambersburg PA
CBHW040303170426
43194CB00021B/2872